Numerology

Reveal the Secret Power of Numbers and Discover How Numerological Divination is Connected to Astrology, Tarot, and Ayurveda

© Copyright 2021

The contents of this book may not be reproduced, duplicated or transmitted without direct written permission from the author.

Under no circumstances will any legal responsibility or blame be held against the publisher for any reparation, damages, or monetary loss due to the information herein, either directly or indirectly.

Legal Notice:

You cannot amend, distribute, sell, use, quote or paraphrase any part or the content within this book without the consent of the author.

Disclaimer Notice:

Please note the information contained within this document is for educational and entertainment purposes only. No warranties of any kind are expressed or implied. Readers acknowledge that the author is not engaging in the rendering of legal, financial, medical or professional advice. Please consult a licensed professional before attempting any techniques outlined in this book.

By reading this document, the reader agrees that under no circumstances are is the author responsible for any losses, direct or indirect, which are incurred as a result of the use of information contained within this document, including, but not limited to, errors, omissions, or inaccuracies.

Your Free Gift (only available for a limited time)

Thanks for getting this book! If you want to learn more about various spirituality topics, then join Mari Silva's community and get a free guided meditation MP3 for awakening your third eye. This guided meditation mp3 is designed to open and strengthen ones third eye so you can experience a higher state of consciousness. Simply visit the link below the image to get started.

https://spiritualityspot.com/meditation

Contents

INTRODUCTION	1
CHAPTER 1: ORIGINS OF NUMEROLOGY	3
History of Numerology	3
How Numerology Works	7
CHAPTER 2: YOUR BIRTH DATE IN NUMBERS	9
Calculating Your Life Path Number	10
Life Path Number 1	11
Life Path Number 2	12
Life Path Number 3	12
Life Path Number 4	13
Life Path Number 5	14
Life Path Number 6	14
Life Path Number 7	15
Life Path Number 8	16
Life Path Number 9	17
Life Path Number 11	17
Life Path Number 22	18
CHAPTER 3: THE NUMEROLOGY OF YOUR NAME	19
Calculating Destiny Number	21
Understanding Destiny Numbers	23
Destiny Number 1	23

- Destiny Number 2 24
- Destiny Number 3 24
- Destiny Number 4 24
- Destiny Number 5 25
- Destiny Number 6 25
- Destiny Number 7 26
- Destiny Number 8 26
- Destiny Number 9 27
- Destiny Number 11 27
- Destiny Number 22 27
- Destiny Number 33 28
- Core Numbers 28

CHAPTER 4: YOUR LIFEPATH PLUS DESTINY NUMBER 31
- Maturity Number 1 32
- Maturity Number 2 33
- Maturity Number 3 33
- Maturity Number 4 34
- Maturity Number 5 34
- Maturity Number 6 35
- Maturity Number 7 36
- Maturity Number 8 36
- Maturity Number 9 37
- Master Maturity Number 11 37
- Master Maturity Number 22 38

CHAPTER 5: DAILY CYCLES AND PATTERNS 39
- Understanding Daily Cycles 39
- Personal Day Number 1 40
- Personal Day Number 2 40
- Personal Day Number 3 41
- Personal Day Number 4 41
- Personal Day Number 5 41
- Personal Day Number 6 41
- Personal Day Number 7 42
- Personal Day Number 8 42

PERSONAL DAY NUMBER 9 42
PERSONAL DAY MASTER NUMBER 11 42
PERSONAL DAY MASTER NUMBER 22 43
UNDERSTANDING AND INTERPRETING THE NUMERICAL PATTERNS 43

CHAPTER 6: THE NINE-YEAR CYCLE 48
CALCULATE YOUR PERSONAL YEAR NUMBER 49
DECIPHERING THE NINE-YEAR CYCLE 49

CHAPTER 7: THE LIFE CYCLE 55
MAJOR LIFE CYCLE NUMBER 1 58
MAJOR LIFE CYCLE NUMBER 2 59
MAJOR LIFE CYCLE NUMBER 3 59
MAJOR LIFE CYCLE NUMBER 4 59
MAJOR LIFE CYCLE NUMBER 5 60
MAJOR LIFE CYCLE NUMBER 6 60
MAJOR LIFE CYCLE NUMBER 7 60
MAJOR LIFE CYCLE NUMBER 8 61
MAJOR LIFE CYCLE NUMBER 9 61
MAJOR LIFE CYCLE NUMBER 11 61
MAJOR LIFE CYCLE NUMBER 22 62

CHAPTER 8: CHARTS AND ARROWS 63
MEANINGS OF FULL ARROWS 65
MEANINGS OF EMPTY ARROWS 68

CHAPTER 9: CALCULATING RELATIONSHIPS 72
RELATIONSHIP NUMBER 1 73
RELATIONSHIP NUMBER 2 74
RELATIONSHIP NUMBER 3 74
RELATIONSHIP NUMBER 4 75
RELATIONSHIP NUMBER 5 75
RELATIONSHIP NUMBER 6 76
RELATIONSHIP NUMBER 7 77
RELATIONSHIP NUMBER 8 77
RELATIONSHIP NUMBER 9 78
RELATIONSHIP NUMBER 11 78
RELATIONSHIP NUMBER 22 79

CHAPTER 10: AYURVEDA AND NUMEROLOGY 80
   VEDIC NUMEROLOGY 82

CHAPTER 11: ASTRO-NUMEROLOGY 87
   CHALLENGES OF LIFE PATH NUMBER 6: DIFFICULTY BEING CONSISTENT 89
   NUMBER 1 - RULED BY THE SUN 90
   NUMBER 2 - RULED BY THE MOON 90
   NUMBER 3 - RULING PLANET: JUPITER 90
   NUMBER 4 - RULING PLANET: URANUS 91
   NUMBER 5 - RULING PLANET: MERCURY 91
   NUMBER 6 - RULING PLANET: VENUS 91
   NUMBER 7 - RULING PLANET: NEPTUNE 92
   NUMBER 8 - RULING PLANET: SATURN 92
   NUMBER 9 - RULING PLANET: MARS 92

CHAPTER 12: TAROT AND NUMEROLOGY 95
   MAJOR ARCANA CARDS 96
   MINOR ARCANA CARDS 101
   THE CONNECTION BETWEEN TAROT AND NUMEROLOGY 106

CONCLUSION 107

HERE'S ANOTHER BOOK BY MARI SILVA THAT YOU MIGHT LIKE 109

YOUR FREE GIFT (ONLY AVAILABLE FOR A LIMITED TIME) 110

REFERENCES 111

Introduction

Do you want to attract more positivity into your life? Do you want to improve any specific aspects of your personal or professional life? Are you curious to get a sneak peek at what life has in store for you? If yes, the answers to these questions lie in numerology.

According to numerology, everything in life can be reduced to a numerical value. All that happens in life and all your interactions with the world can be recorded in numerical terms. You may have discovered certain numbers resonate with you. You might consider some to be lucky or even attach a sentimental value to them. For instance, your loved ones' birthdate or even your birth date can hold significance. Certain numbers may remind you of something special such as your anniversary, the day you got your first job or any other special occasion. From the prices of goods to anything you come across in life, everything has a specific number.

Consciously or subconsciously, the entire world is governed by numbers in one way or another. Numerology is the science of understanding the connection between numbers and your life. By learning about numerology, you can learn about your inner motivations and discover your true self. You can also learn about what motivates you and others. Think about all the benefits you can gain by doing this - from making better decisions to reconnecting with your inner self, numerology plays an important role in all aspects of your life. It allows you to analyze different personalities, discover your inner affinities, and make the most of the opportunities that present themselves in your life. This is not a new concept but has been around for thousands of years. Time and again, science has also proved the benefits of numerology.

The uncertainties of the future can make life a little overwhelming. In such instances, getting a sneak peek of all that destiny has in store for you can be helpful. Well, if you are eager to do this, it is time to learn about numerology. The good news is everything you need to know is provided in this book. This book will act as your guide every step of the way.

In this book, you will learn about the origins of numerology and how it works with your personal birth date, and the numerology of your name. You will learn about the theoretical aspects of numerology and how you can calculate your life path number, destiny number and how they are related. From daily cycles and patterns to the nine-year cycle, you will understand what's in store for you. You will learn the role numerology plays in your love life and relationships with others. Once you are well versed in all these basic topics, this book teaches you to create a chart using all this information. It also introduces you to the relationship between numerology and Ayurveda, tarot and astrology.

So, are you eager to get started on this journey of self-discovery by using numerology? Do you want to uncover any hidden talents or opportunities that will help you to fulfill your destiny? Let's get started!

Chapter 1: Origins of Numerology

Numbers not only hold a numerical value but spiritual value too. Numerology helps demystify the relationship between numbers and their personal energies. Numerology is also considered as the study of the numerical values associated with different letters of the alphabet. If you are familiar with the imaginary world of Harry Potter, you may know that arithmancy was Hermione Granger's favorite subject. Even though many details aren't included about arithmancy in the series, it can be inferred that it involves the magical properties of numbers. Hermione often uses several complex charts and divination to predict the future using numbers. Numerology is the real-life equivalent of arithmancy.

History of Numerology

Numerologists believe numbers influence everything that happens in the world. Everything depends on their mystical properties. All their perceived mystical properties result from the energy vibration inherent to numbers. Vibration is the term commonly used by new-age practitioners to describe the inherent power in certain items such as gemstones, colors, essential oils and crystals. It is not just crystals and gemstones that have energy, but even numbers do.

In numerology, it is believed that every number has a unique vibration that gives it special properties. These properties can be used to understand an individual's behavior or even predict compatibility in relationships. Numerological analysis can determine an individual's lucky number or days. Recurring numbers can be used to obtain clues about how the world works and the significance of different individuals or events in one's life. Numerologists strongly believe there is no such thing as an accident. Everything that happens ultimately boils down to numbers.

The ideas of numerology are not new concepts. The earliest records of numerology date to ancient Egypt, Babylon, China, Japan, Rome and Greece. Pythagoras is credited with the creation of the system of numerology. He was an ancient Greek philosopher born in 569 BC. Historians know only a little about this famous philosopher because most of his original work did not survive the test of time. Also, the historical mentions of Pythagoras were written by individuals who came hundreds of years after his time. This is one reason why some historians believe the discoveries often attributed to Pythagoras were created by his followers later.

The followers of Pythagoras are known as Pythagoreans. Pythagoras studied music, philosophy and mathematics comprehensively. One of the most important discoveries associated with the Pythagorean School of thinking is the Pythagorean Theorem. According to this theorem, in any right-angled triangle, the square of the hypotenuse's length is always equal to the sum of the other two sides' squares. Does this ring any bells? The Pythagorean Theorem is summed as $a2 + b2 = c2$. This is one of the basic mathematical theorems taught in school. Pythagoreans are also believed to be the ones who discovered the first irrational number or the Pythagoras' constant - the square root of two.

Besides these discoveries, Pythagoras and Pythagoreans also believed that numbers have inherent mystical properties. This belief stems from the discovery that adding up a series of odd numbers, starting with 1, results in the square of the concerned number. These discoveries further strengthened the belief of Pythagoreans that "all is numbers." It essentially means that everything in the world can be measured and described numerically and in proportions. The "all is numbers" belief also suggests the world is purely made of numbers, and everything can be reduced to a numerical value. Well, this idea is logical, and it has a significant influence on math and science.

While studying mathematical concepts, Pythagoreans sorted all numbers into different categories. For instance, numbers such as 1, 4 and 9 are squares because the corresponding number of pebbles or dots can be arranged in the shape of a perfect square. Likewise, 1, 3, 6 and 10 are triangular because the corresponding pebbles or dots can be arranged into shapes of regular triangles. Another observation is that numbers such as 2, 6 and 12 are oblong because, when arranged, the corresponding number of pebbles will form rectangles.

Pythagoreans not only described numbers in mathematical and geometrical terms but also according to their non-numerical traits. These traits have little to do with science or math and are more to do with intuition and mysticism. For instance, even numbers were considered feminine, while odd numbers were thought of as masculine. The number one is associated with creativity since adding multiples of one often creates another number. Similarly, number two is feminine and represents duality, while three is all about masculinity. A combination of two and three represents marriage because it is the midpoint of numbers one through nine. It also represents justice. Ten is believed to be a sacred number because it is the sum of the first four digits. These beliefs helped to create ten fundamental opposites such as odd and even, right and left, masculine and feminine, straighten crooked, light and darkness, square and oblong, good and evil, one and many and odd and even.

The interest in mathematical mysticism increased after Pythagoras's death. It quickly gained prominence in the form of neo-Pythagoreans during the first century A.D., but the interest in the non-mathematical theories proposed by Pythagoras soon faded away. During the late 1800s, several books about the concept of number vibration, music and colors were published by Mrs. L Dow Balliett. Several other writers might have published their works before her, but it was her books that brought to light the relationship between Pythagorean principles and other concepts used in modern numerology.

A general philosophy followed by all numerologists is that every number has a specific vibration. It's not just numbered, but people, places, food and even objects tend to have their own vibrations. For instance, certain places, people and foods make us happy. Why does this happen? It happens due to the constant flow and exchange of energy in the universe. To live a happy, harmonious and productive life, we all must ensure our environment vibrates in sync with our energies. It is not just numerology that concentrates on this vibration of energies. Some new-age practices believe this vibration results from the movement of subatomic particles.

Certain schools of numerology believe this vibration results from the music of spheres. It essentially backs the Pythagorean belief that celestial bodies make a specific sound while orbiting the Earth, but this belief was disproved by science because the Earth and other planets orbit around the sun, and it isn't the other way around. This is where modern numerology makes up for the flaws present in the Pythagorean concept of numerology. Modern numerologists use numbers to make sense of the universe instead of relying on intangible concepts.

How Numerology Works

In life, there are no such things as accidents. It might seem as if your birth date and name are seemingly random, but they have deeper meanings and reasons. Numerology is a treasure chest filled with helpful information. By understanding the hidden meanings of numbers, you'll have the key to unlock the treasure chest.

Numbers hold a special significance in certain religions too. For instance, in Christianity, the number 888 is believed to be the representation of Jesus, while 666 is considered the number of the beast. Let us not forget about the holy trinity or that Hanukkah lasts for eight nights. According to Chinese tradition, number four is believed to bring bad luck. The system of numerology is used in modern times to discover the hidden meanings of the world.

Most use numerology like astrology. We use it to predict the future and as a tool for self-discovery. A common reason people turn to numerology is that it helps them understand their life's purpose. Life can be confusing and overwhelming. By calculating your life path and destiny number, you can learn more about your characteristics, unique personality traits and even weaknesses. These numbers can remind yourself of your true purpose in life, finding the ideal profession and creating healthier relationships. You will learn more about calculating these numbers in the later chapters.

Numerology can also help you make better decisions and choices in life. Every decision you make changes the course of your life. By choosing a path that matches your numerology chart, it becomes easier to create a life that's happy, fulfilling and rewarding.

Numerological readings can establish and maintain healthier and happier relationships. Knowing more about yourself and the personality traits of others in your life makes it easier to maintain relationships. When you understand all this, it becomes simple to form and maintain positive and lasting ties. A solid understanding of your basic traits makes it easier to manage any expectations in a relationship.

Your life path number helps you understand your strengths, weaknesses, and other personality traits. It also determines any favorable or unfavorable periods. It comes in handy while preparing and planning for important events in your life, such as changing your career or embarking on new relationships. Similarly, your destiny number can reveal what you will do in life. The destiny number combines the numerical values associated with the alphabet of your full name. A combination of one's destiny and life path number can be used to make important decisions.

Since numerology gives you a better understanding of yourself and life in general, it becomes easier to deal with any obstacles that happen during your life. Likewise, it makes you more aware of all the potential opportunities.

Chapter 2: Your Birth Date in Numbers

If you are working hard to improve your life, it means you are moving a step closer to your goals every day, but the lack of important information about your life path number may be holding you back. By using numerology, you can get a better understanding of yourself. If you are new to the world of numerology, you have likely heard about different strengths associated with life path numbers. Good and bad are two sides of the same coin. This balance is the rule of nature, so every life path number not only has certain strengths but weaknesses too.

It becomes easier to overcome challenges caused by the shadow side of your life path number by understanding them through numerology. The life path number is based on your date of birth, and can determine your life's purpose while giving you better clarity about the different opportunities available. In this section, you will learn how to calculate your life path number and different exercises you can follow to overcome any weaknesses associated with that.

Calculating Your Life Path Number

To harness the power of numerology, it is important to determine your life path number. No worries – it's incredibly simple to calculate. It is essentially the sum of your full birth date. It is a representation of who you are at the moment of your birth. It also helps determine your personality traits, drawbacks, and different talents. To get started with calculating your life path number, you only need your birth date. It includes the date, month and year in which you were born. The next step is to convert all the numbers into single digits. For instance, if you were born on 17th February, you need to add 1 and 7, which gives you 8. There is one important consideration while doing this. All numbers need to be converted into single digits except the numbers 11 and 22. For instance, if you were born on 11th February, leave the number as it is. Remember this rule because it applies to birthdays that fall on the 22nd of a month or the total of digits, which end up in 11 or 22. In numerology, 11 and 22 are considered *Master Numbers*.

Here is a simple example to get a better understanding of how to calculate your life path number. Let us assume that you were born on 22nd November 1994.

November 11th (month) - 11

22nd (date) - 4 (2 + 2)

1994 (year) - 23 (1 + 9 + 9 + 4)

Now, add all these numbers and you end up with 38. So, the life path number in this case will be 11 (3+8).

For instance, if someone was born on the 10th March 1980, the date and month will be 1 and 3, respectively. By adding all the individual digits in the birth year, you will arrive at 9 (1 + 9 + 8 + 0). There are three single-digit numbers associated with the individual's date, month and year of birth, which are 1, 3 and 9, respectively. Now, it is time to add all these numbers until you are left with a single-digit number. The sum of all these numbers is 13. So, the life path number is 4 (1 + 3).

Do you realize how simple it is to calculate your life path number? Now you know how to do this, so the next step is to understand each number's strengths and weaknesses.

Life Path Number 1

Individuals with life path number 1 are creative and dedicated. It essentially means you have an inherent tendency to stick to your goals without getting distracted by other things. The most effective techniques that can attract more positivity into your life are visualization and creating a dream board. On the downside, those with this number care too much about others' needs, desires and opinions, so you probably might be trying to achieve goals that don't mean anything to you. Your inherent desire to please others takes away the courage required to live the life you want.

Suitable Exercises

The simplest way to overcome the weaknesses associated with this number is to concentrate on activities that help you get in touch with your personal values. For instance, take some time and list five things that mean the most to you. These things need to add value to your life, even if it means you gain no praise from others or are subjected to external criticism. Once you have this list, ask yourself what different goals can be set to live by your personal values. Anything that is not in sync with your values adds no real meaning to your life. The activities you need to concentrate on are the ones that hold to your values. Use your creativity and dedication to become more confident, independent and autonomous to live a life you desire without worrying about others.

Life Path Number 2

Individuals with life path number two are genuine, sensitive and extremely honest. Tuning in to their heart's desires and emotions is quite easy for them. On the downside, they can feel dejected and hopeless when faced with criticism and difficulties in life. Instead of looking for solutions to the problems or obstacles, you end up wallowing in negativity about all the possible things that can go wrong in any situation. This fear can prevent you from taking the desired action to achieve your goals.

Suitable Exercises

To overcome the challenges associated with life path number two, concentrate on developing and maintaining a positive mindset. To let go of your negativity, ask yourself where the negative thoughts stem from. What does your inner voice say, and where do you think it comes from? Perhaps it is a teacher, a friend, a family member, or even a mentor. Make a note of the different self-defeating beliefs and assumptions that play in a loop within your mind. Try to reframe all negative thoughts into positive ones. For instance, instead of thinking, "I cannot do this," or "I am not good enough," reframe it as "I cannot do it right now," or "I am capable of achieving my goals." Question your negative thoughts instead of accepting them as the absolute truth. The shadow side of this number brings lethargy, so try to elevate your energy levels and adopt a positive mindset.

Life Path Number 3

Individuals with life path number three are blessed with a socially magnetic personality. Whether it is networking, personal relationships, or anything else that involves others, you have a significant advantage over others. These individuals are optimistic and filled with inherent positivity that help them achieve their goals. On the flip side, they can be uncertain and have a tough time with commitment. Finding one thing to concentrate on and achieving it can become challenging for those with life path number three, so you must try to devote all your energy toward one goal instead of several goals at once.

Suitable Exercises

Since life path number three comes with a shadow side of difficulty with commitment and focus, mindfulness is a great way to ensure that you stay in the moment. It allows you to concentrate and focus on only one thing at a time. The simplest way to do this is by concentrating on your breathing. Spend around 10-15 minutes daily focusing on your breathing and nothing else. Don't worry about anything and allow your thoughts to drift. By staying in the moment, it becomes easier to focus on one task instead of unnecessarily squandering your energy through multitasking.

Life Path Number 4

Individuals with life path number four are practical and have a strong will. These know what they want and come up with a practical plan to achieve their goals. On the downside, since they are so focused on what they want, their perspective is rigid. This rigidity prevents them from seeing any opportunities that come their way. They may also struggle with manifesting wealth into their lives.

Suitable Exercises

The good news is managing and manifesting wealth into your life is not a difficult task. A simple way is to use the Law of Attraction to determine what you need the finances for, the desired quantity and concentrating on Earth. From visualizing the financial success you desire to daily affirmations, there are several techniques you can use. By thinking and maintaining a positive attitude and beliefs about money to expel negative beliefs, it becomes easier to obtain the financial success you want.

Life Path Number 5

Individuals born with a life path number five are open-minded, creative and flexible with out-of-the-box thinking and solutions. Instead of worrying about the future or past, you are good at staying in the moment and aware of current experiences. The shadow side of this can make them self-indulgent, concentrate only on transient pleasures of life, and not see the bigger picture. It is important to not only maintain a positive attitude about yourself, but it is equally important to project this positivity toward others in your life.

Suitable Exercises

Since this life path number can make you self-focused, it will do you good to think about others. Instead of worrying about your own goals and dreams, try to do your bit for others. A random act of kindness with no expectation is a great way to bring balance to your life, so make it a point to do one good deed daily. It can be something as simple as grabbing a coffee for a coworker or talking to your friend when they need you. Once you focus on the bigger picture and not just your own life, you will automatically feel better. Stay in the present, but if everything you do is chasing transient pleasures, you will attain nothing significant or meaningful. Think and plan for the future without letting go of your inherent mindfulness.

Life Path Number 6

Life path number six is associated with compassion and generosity. These are individuals who spread goodness wherever they go. They are blessed with a nurturing nature and high levels of energy. A combination of these factors makes it easier to maintain the right kind of positive attitude in life. The shadow side of number six makes it difficult to balance giving and receiving. If all you ever do is give and then give more, you will have nothing left for yourself. It can also make it increasingly difficult to concentrate on the things you love and cherish.

Suitable Exercises

Since these individuals are nurturers and givers, it is important to concentrate on self-care. What good can you be to others if you cannot help yourself? Remember, even safety instructions in flights suggest you need to put on your own oxygen mask before helping others. Let go of the little voice in your head that tells you it is selfish to look after yourself. Prioritizing self-care is not selfish and is a sign of self-love and compassion. Ensure that your deeds add value to your life before helping others.

A simple way to do this is by listing different things you appreciate about yourself. Don't let these traits be determined by what you can do for others. For instance, some traits you can include are creativity, dynamic and helping nature, or even good listening skills. This list will act as a reminder of your self-worth. The next step is to concentrate on doing the things you love and enjoy. This is the only way you can add value to your life. By concentrating on yourself, you can increase your self-esteem, self-respect and establish healthy personal boundaries.

Life Path Number 7

Individuals with life path number seven are peace loving and have serene energy radiating from within. They are reflective, too, and adept at maintaining bonds with others without letting it define their lives. Maintaining and nourishing healthy and well-balanced relationships is your secret power. On the flip side, they may struggle to appreciate all the good in their life.

Suitable Exercises

To let go of this number's shadow side, it takes a conscious effort to connect with your intuition and spirituality instead of solely depending on the analytical aspect of your mind. Maintaining a gratitude journal and meditating are two simple activities to bring about a sense of positivity to your life and mind. Every day makes a note of at least 3-5 things you are grateful for. This is an effective way to let go of any negativity you might harbor while focusing on the silver lining in all the obstacles you face, but doing this will take conscious time, energy and effort. With practice, you will get better at doing this.

Life Path Number 8

Individuals with life path number eight are incredibly determined, focused, and thoughtful. They are also practical and confident, which makes them great at organizing. The shadow side of this life path number means the practicality you desire leaves little or no room for dreaming. It can also make it difficult to connect with your emotional side because your analytical mind rules your life. These individuals are also susceptible to concentrating too much on materialistic possessions that leaves no room for emotional value, so cultivating and maintaining lasting love isn't always easy for them.

Suitable Exercises

The simplest way to overcome the weaknesses associated with this life path number is by connecting with your emotions. Don't ignore or repress them, but allow yourself to feel whatever you feel. There is no judgment here, so stop ignoring your needs. Once you accept your emotions and determine their source, any discomfort associated with them goes away. It is time to go back to the basics and concentrate on every emotion. What do you feel about different emotions? What caused these emotions? How were you conditioned to deal with your emotions? By answering these questions, you get a better idea of what your emotions mean and why you feel the way you do. It allows you to connect with your true feelings to better understand your wants, needs and desires in life. How can you achieve your goals if you are uncertain of what you want or why?

Life Path Number 9

Individuals with life path number 9 are quite honorable and blessed with a sense of fairness. These traits make others automatically respect them. They are also incredibly charismatic and have magnetic personalities. By learning to harness this magnetism, they can attract all the good they desire in life. The only problem is the 9's shadow side can prevent them from doing this. These individuals can develop an unhealthy obsession with achieving success in their lives or attaining financial freedom. The negative thoughts they have about the things they desire effectively prevent them from attaining their goals.

Suitable Exercises

The first step toward overcoming the weaknesses associated with this number is to acknowledge your beliefs. If there are any negative beliefs about the things you truly desire in life, it's time to reform the beliefs that prevent you from succeeding. A simple activity you can follow is to note a specific goal you have in life. After this, surround this word with as many positive beliefs and associations as you can. For instance, if finances are important to you, you can write good associations such as "It will let me travel as much as I want," "It allows me the freedom to experiment," or "It means I don't have to worry about my future." By doing this, you are essentially manifesting your thoughts into reality. You are trying to attract the positively required to attain your goals without faltering along the way.

Life Path Number 11

The life path number 11 is one of the master numbers and numerology. Individuals with this number are blessed with spiritual awareness. Others might perceive them to be someone who knows more than they do. They also have a special gift of insight. They have plenty to offer to the world around and always dream big. On the shadow side, they are prone to severe mood swings and swing between extremes in life. They also struggle to feel grateful for all the good they have in life.

Suitable Exercises

The most effective and straightforward means to overcome the weaknesses of the shadow side of this life path number is by concentrating on emotional balance. Learn to shut down the inner critic in your head to manifest your true desires. The simplest way to do this is through meditation. Through meditation, you can calm your mind, stay in the moment and pursue your dreams and desires. Instead of allowing your emotions to guide the way, learn to manage your emotions.

Life Path Number 22

The other Master Number is 22. It is believed to be the most powerful life path number of all. These individuals are blessed with a powerhouse of positive energy, which can make the world a better place. Even though it is a powerful number, it comes with its own set of challenges. It is highly unlikely they are negative, but they can become overbearing and self-censored. These traits increase the risk of self-sabotage and prevent you from reading the life you desire.

Suitable Exercises

Become mindful of how you communicate with yourself and others in general. Learn to strike a balance between being insincere and tactless. By expressing your authentic self, it becomes easier to achieve your goals and dreams. For instance, list all the things you struggle to say. After this, it's time to look for how you can say them without hurting yourself or others. Personal development exercises can help you overcome the challenges associated with this number and free up more space for yourself and all that you want in life.

Chapter 3: The Numerology of Your Name

There is no such thing as an accident in this life. Everything that has happened, is happening, and will happen is all the manifestation of destiny's work. What do you use every day but never pay for? Time to put on your thinking hats. Well, do you know the answer to this riddle? If you don't, the answer is your name. We use our names daily but never pay for them. Often people think, "What's in a name?" Well, your name is not an accident. Even if it seems like something you were bestowed with at birth, it shapes the course of your destiny. Every letter of your name actively shapes your reality.

Remember, in the previous chapters; it was mentioned that every number has a specific vibration? Since every letter of the alphabet corresponds with a specific number, your name has a unique vibration; it is the true reflection of your life's purpose. The vibrations associated with it helps shape your unique personality and perception of life. As with your birthdate, even your name is of utmost importance in numerology.

In the previous chapter, you were introduced to the concept of life path numbers and the different traits associated with them. Now, it is time to add another tool to your numerology toolbox- the Destiny number. Sometimes, certain qualities associated with your life path number correspond perfectly with your personality, but there will be certain parts that don't make complete sense. If that's the case, it means you are missing some vital information. Your destiny or expression number provides this vital information. The destiny number or expression number is an important aspect of numerology and it complements the life path number.

The life path number offers a one-dimensional projection of who you are. The name suggests it helps identify the primary purpose of your life. Once you combine this number with the destiny number, it helps you understand how you will achieve your purpose projected by the life path number. When you combine these two ingredients, it helps create a complete profile of who you are and how to achieve your destiny.

For instance, if your life path number is one, then you are a go-getter. This number is associated with originality, creativity, leadership, initiation, competition, action and immense confidence. By placing your destiny number on top of the life path number, you understand how you can achieve the purpose set out by life path number one. The destiny number essentially sets the bar you need to live up to. It is similar to any expectations you might have of yourself or other people's expectations of you. It essentially offers insight into how an individual will express his purpose set out by the life path number.

Let's go ahead with the previous example of life path number one. If the destiny number is two, you might experience certain internal conflicts because number one is about independence, leadership, achievement and individuality. But destiny number two is all about harmony, love, balance and paying attention to group dynamics. Do you see how the basic traits associated with these numbers can create conflict? But it does not mean these numbers are an impossible combination. Instead, every combination comes with its own set of brilliant potential and strengths.

The only thing you need to do is understand how you can maximize and increase your strength associated with each number while reducing any weaknesses so they work in harmony. When you know your life's purpose, it is important to understand how you can achieve that purpose.

The destiny number helps reveal more about your life's purpose. It offers insight into how you need to live your life and all the different things you need to do to achieve your purpose.

Since it offers this insight, it becomes easier to note all the different opportunities that might present themselves in your life. It's not just opportunities, but it also helps identify any potential obstacles or hurdles you need to overcome to manifest your life's purpose. It helps understand what your destiny is and how to achieve and express your true purpose. Another benefit of understanding the destiny numbers is that they enable you to make the most of all the life experiences. Showing you the bigger picture, and the things you need to do to get there, makes you more mindful.

Calculating Destiny Number

Do you want to learn how to calculate your destiny number? If yes, grab a sheet of paper and write down your full name that you were given at birth. Don't forget to write all of your middle names – if you have more than one. One rule to remember is you can skip the Jr., Second, Third or any other suffixes.

According to numerology, every letter of the alphabet corresponds with a specific number. This number is determined by the positioning of the number in the alphabet. For instance, the letter Q is the 17th letter, and the number it corresponds with is 8 (1+7). If this sounds too cumbersome, create a chart using the positioning of each number. Here are the different letters and their corresponding numbers.

A, J, S = 1
B, K, T = 2
C, L, U = 3
D, M, V = 4
E, N, W = 5
F, O, X = 6
G, P, Y = 7
H, Q, Z = 8
I, R = 9

Here is a simple example to give you a better understanding of how to calculate your expression or destiny number by using all the letters of your full name (birth name). Let us calculate the destiny number of John Winston Lennon.

The first step is to break down the full name into the different numbers the letters are associated with.

JOHN WINSTON LENNON

So, the name John corresponds with the numbers 1, 6, 8 and 5, respectively. By adding these single-digit numbers, you get 20. Whenever required, add the numbers to ensure you obtain a single-digit number. The number associated with John is 2 (2+0). Repeat this step for calculating the numbers associated with Winston and Lennon in this example. The calculations are:

John = 2 (1 + 6 + 8 + 5)

Winston = 33 (5 + 9 + 5 + 1 + 2 + 6 + 5)

Lennon = 11 (3 + 5 +5 + 5 + 6 + 5)

Note: While calculating the destiny numbers, you shouldn't reduce the master numbers (11, 22 and 33) to single digits but should leave them as they are.

Now that you have the individual numbers associated with the individual's first, middle and last name, it is time to calculate the expression number. The expression number is the summation of all these numbers. John Winston Lennon's expression number is 46 (2 + 33 + 11). This can be further reduced to 10, which gives the expression number 1 (1 + 0).

Understanding Destiny Numbers

In this section, let's look at the strengths and challenges associated with it. In life, we can all use a little extra advantage. You can get this advantage by understanding yourself, your purpose – and how to manifest this purpose. To do this, you need to have an in-depth knowledge of your strengths, weaknesses and any potential challenges you need to overcome. So, let's learn more about all this.

Destiny Number 1

Creativity, entrepreneurship, and leadership traits are associated with this number. Destiny number 1s are destined for greatness and authority in whichever field they choose. Achieving independence, trusting your creativity and turning your ideas into reality are things you strive for in life. The confidence to transform your dreams into reality increases as you mature and grow.

On the downside you might not have the required confidence to follow your ideas, especially when stuck dealing with authorities. It can be difficult to sit by and watch as others get all the opportunities you feel you deserve. Learn to harness your inner leadership skills while honing your listening skills to shatter glass ceilings like you dream of doing.

Destiny Number 2

Individuals with destiny number 2 are blessed with a strong sense of intuition, are natural healers and value relationships deeply. They strive to create a life filled with beauty, peace and harmony. Whether it is your personal or professional life, partnerships hold a special appeal. On the flip side, you might give too much of yourself to others so you have nothing left. Instead of the world around, concentrate on the world within, and focus on your dreams and aspirations. Learn to use your natural empathy by tuning into your intuition.

Destiny Number 3

Everyone is drawn to their charismatic and magnetic personality and a smile that lights up the room. These individuals are inherently optimistic, and their joyous and creative personality acts as a people magnet. Their strengths include self-expression and the ability to express their thoughts effectively and efficiently. Your sensitivity that can be your strength can quickly become a weakness too. This sensitivity increases self-doubt and prompts self-criticism. The only way to move ahead is by letting go of your inner critic, who induces self-doubt.

Destiny Number 4

Individuals with this destiny number are honest, hardworking, blessed with leadership qualities and dependable. You love passionately, and your love knows no bounds. There isn't anything you wouldn't do for your loved ones, especially family. Working toward success and leading others comes naturally to you due to your entrepreneurial abilities. All the good that's within you wish to share with others. Unfortunately, you stand the risk of burning yourself out while trying to help others. Remember, even when you intend to help others, offering unnecessary advice and telling others what to do can make you seem bossy and domineering. Try to use your natural traits to help attain your goals while working with others as a team.

Destiny Number 5

Individuals with destiny number 5 value their freedom more than anything else. They are naturally talented, creative and have multiple areas of interest. A charming personality, curious nature, a need to explore and wonderful storytelling abilities make them attractive to others. Since you are drawn toward multiple things, settling with one option might not appeal to you. This can make your life seem more complicated than it needs to be. Learning to focus on a single task without getting distracted is one skill you need to learn. Remember, being with someone doesn't mean less freedom for you. All that matters is how you deal with relationships in life. By setting and implementing personal boundaries, holding onto your love for freedom is easy.

Destiny Number 6

This destiny number makes you feel a strong sense of responsibility toward others, especially your loved ones. You detest the thought of letting anyone down. You desire success coupled with harmony and peace. These individuals have a strong inclination toward a perfectionist attitude, and everything needs to be the absolute best. This stands true especially when you lend others a helping hand. The only problem with this destiny number is you tend to do things for others at your own expense. Let go of your perfectionist attitude to get anywhere in life. No one is good at everything, and we all need help occasionally.

Destiny Number 7

Individuals with this destiny number have a keen sense of seeking truth in any situation. You are insightful, and the way your mind works is similar to an X-ray. Your brilliant sense of intuition, coupled with an understanding of the universe's mystic ways, ensures you are always on the right track. These individuals require a career that allows them to work independently to make the most of their sharp mind and intuition. On the downside, it might not always be easy to trust yourself. The only way to get over this is by learning to trust your intuition. If your internal voice says something is amiss about a situation, it's probably right.

Destiny Number 8

This destiny number belongs to all the individuals capable of seeing the bigger picture. While most of us are overwhelmed by the little things in life, they step back and understand the role they play. They love to be in charge of things, usually form the upper rung of management, and are good at managing resources. Status, money and power are a few things you long to be comfortable with. Once you understand your destiny as a leader, managing the resources available at your disposal becomes easier.

If you feel unworthy of your achievements, it's not just the wins you need to prepare yourself for, but the losses too. Even when it feels like you have no control over your life, you do. By improving your self-worth, you can automatically feel better about yourself and your purpose in life. It also brings you a step closer to your destiny while eliminating self-sabotaging beliefs.

Destiny Number 9

These individuals are natural counselors, teachers and blessed with a deep sense of intuition. Their deep intuition, coupled with wisdom and spiritual insight, draws others to them. You always stand up for the underdog and use your spiritual gift to share success with others. On the downside, you probably give too much to others or don't receive enough for all the effort you make. You have an inherent desire to be of service to others, and it can leave you exhausted and tired, so an important lesson these individuals need to learn is that life is not just about giving but receiving too.

Destiny Number 11

This destiny number is considered spiritual. You have the power required to manifest your dreams into reality. As a natural-born leader and spiritual teacher, you can use your words to inspire others. Your magnetic persona automatically draws people toward you. Once you let your intuition guide the way, you will become unstoppable.

It becomes easy to doubt yourself because of your fine-tuned vision. 11 is a master number and so it comes with great potential and challenges. Don't doubt your vision for the future; listen to your gut and let it guide the way. You can use meditation to calm your mind and strengthen your intuition.

Destiny Number 22

This is a master number that brings with it an enormous potential to manifest your goals into reality. You have an inherent drive to leave behind a legacy that will help generations to come and not just the existing one. Incredible intuition and practical nature are two important traits that help attain the success you desire, not just in the physical realm but also in the spiritual one. You want to lay down the foundations for not just your family but wish to do something good for the world in general. This destiny number is a master builder and a natural teacher.

There is a lot of potential within you, but this potential also comes with its own set of challenges. When you want to help so many people, it's easy to feel as if you are responsible for them all. This can quickly become overwhelming and consume you. It is okay to want to help others, but it is equally okay to let others help too. To be successful, concentrate on your self-discipline and patience. Also, don't forget to look after your physical and emotional wellbeing.

Destiny Number 33

As with destiny numbers 11 and 22, this one is different from all the other single-digit numbers. Individuals with this number showcase quality similar to the numbers 3 and 6. You are creative, expressive and talented and wish to transform the world. Selflessness, generosity, energy and artistic inclination are defining traits of these individuals. They have a maternal vibration and are natural caregivers. You are also perceptive, kind and intuitive, but your desire to help others can quickly drain you of your energy. You might also face certain challenges with self-expression. Since number 6 is deeply associated with service, you might believe others need your attention more than you do. This distracts you from understanding and believing in yourself.

Core Numbers

Let's look at certain core numbers everyone needs to be aware of. You cannot make the most of numerology's various benefits until you learn how to understand the different numbers.

The first number you need to understand is the life path number. Perhaps this is one of the most important numbers you will ever calculate and use in numerology. It is derived from your date of birth. This reveals some vital information about the ideal direction for you and life and all the different lessons you must learn. It essentially provides a very broad outline of all the different opportunities and challenges that await you. It also gives better insight into your personality traits that will help make this journey easier and fruitful. To calculate the life part number, you need to add the different digits that make up your birth date.

The expression number is the second number you learn to calculate after the life part number. It is derived from all the different numbers present in the letters of your full name. Your full name is the name you were given during birth. It includes no suffixes. The expression number is used to get a better understanding of your talents and abilities that have been present since your birth. It is also known as the destiny number or the potential number.

The heart's desire number is calculated by adding the different vowels present in your full name. Once again, the name we are referring to is the name you were given at birth. It helps get a better insight into your souls' deepest desires, likes and dislikes and everything else you keep private.

The personality number is calculated by adding all the consonants in your full birth name. All your surface traits are revealed by this number. It offers information about how you like to dress, your sense of style and how you usually interact with others.

Another number calculated using your birth name is the hereditary number. It is the sum of all letters present in your last name. The last name is also known as the family name or surname. It offers insight into your passive personality traits. It essentially refers to the traits shared by family members and is a part of your heritage. Understanding this number makes it easier to ensure your energy vibrates in sync with that of your family members.

The growth number is the sum of all the letters of your first name. The growth number often acts as a modifier to the life path number. It helps identify a pattern that promotes your growth and development in life. You can use this information to develop the required skills required to ensure you are on track, revealed by your life path number.

Chapter 4: Your Lifepath Plus Destiny Number

We all have a maturity number in numerology. The energy associated with this number manifests itself when we enter our 40s. It is a little fascinating and surprising that everything in numerology has a precise calculation and the maturity number is the only exception. The energy, manifestation, and the influence of this appear gradually. You can see it by the ages of 35- 50. It's quite similar to driving down on a highway and seeing all the billboards. While you navigate life following your life path number, the maturity number gives you a better understanding of your final destination. This helps you understand where you are heading – whether or not you fully realize it.

Since this usually manifests itself as a midlife message, it might feel like you hit a transformation or changing point. In some ways, this number is a precise indication of your true self. After you have completed the first phase of life, the years associated with all thoughts of "been there and done that," the second part begins. The maturity number guides this portion. It's a common belief in the community of numerologists that the maturity number isn't in full force until an individual reaches 50 years of age.

A defining characteristic of the maturity number is that you are suddenly filled with additional energy. This energy can make you feel as if you don't have sufficient time or the patience required to waste on things that aren't propelling you toward your goal. This is one reason why individuals experience life-changing moments once they enter the 30s. You don't have to worry about it because it is your maturity number at play.

It is quite easy to calculate your maturity number. It is the summation of your life path number and destiny or expression number. Here is a quick recap of how your life path and destiny numbers are calculated. Add all the numbers in your birthdate to obtain the life path number. The destiny or expression number is the sum of all the numbers corresponding with the letters in your full birth name. Don't hesitate to refer to the detailed steps discussed in the previous chapter for these calculations. Once you have both of these, merely add them to obtain your maturity number.

The maturity number is also known as the realization of a real number. For instance, if your life path number is 5 and your destiny number is 9, your maturity number is 5 (5 + 9 = 14, 1 + 4 = 5). Now, it is important you understand more about each of the maturity numbers.

Maturity Number 1

This number is associated with independence, so individuals with this maturity number are often reevaluating their idea of independence and know what it means to stand on their feet. It encourages you to take the initiative, step into the role of a leader, and take on calculated risks to achieve your goals and passions. The one area where this maturity number will challenge you, includes situations when the need for independence takes precedence over everything else.

Sometimes, your sense of independence or dependence is highlighted. It also influences how you connect and relate to those around you. Are you wondering what all this might look like for you in life? Well, you must reevaluate your self-centered behaviors. Don't ignore your inherent desire to break free of any situations where you are dependent on others. This maturity number brings with it a dramatic change in your financial situations due to life transitions such as illness, divorce, or anything else along these lines.

Maturity Number 2

This maturity number essentially suggests you are reevaluating your emotional sensitivity so it benefits you and others. It means life is calling you to make the most of your diplomacy. It encourages you to contribute toward creating and maintaining healthy relationships, and to get involved with others and work in groups. The primary challenge associated with this number is it sheds light on all issues associated with your sensitivity. Sometimes, your sense of self in a relationship is called into question; you need to modulate your oversensitivity and concentrate on maintaining healthy relationships.

Now is the time for self-introspection to understand if you have been insensitive to others. Self-centered behaviors that might hurt others are undesirable. Try to look beyond yourself and become a part of groups to contribute to the greater good. Understand that yourself worth stems from within, and you don't need external approval. So, stop being a doormat for others.

Maturity Number 3

This number indicates you are trying to understand what it means to be expressive, filled with joy and creativity. It encourages you to embrace your creativity, spend more time with others and learn to express yourself. The most common obstacles faced by those with this maturity number are associated with creativity that suddenly takes center stage. Situations could challenge your ability to enjoy life, communicate effectively, interact with others and your sense of enthusiasm.

The best way to break free of all these things is by expressing yourself through artistic means. The sky's the limit, and there are various forms of self-expression you can use, such as writing, dancing, singing and other art forms. Understand that life comes with its own set of emotional ups and downs, and you need only to live through them. Once you live your life in alignment with your creative self-expression, luck, comfort and abundance will enter your life.

Maturity Number 4

Understanding what it means to work with limitations is what this maturity number is about. It essentially means this number is guiding you to work effectively and efficiently to reach your goals, create systems and processes which will help you again the goals, and leave a legacy that adds value to this world. Any issue associated with limitation and restriction is commonly associated with this maturity number. Sometimes, you need to change your attitude and become more optimistic while tackling the situation one step at a time. Instead of getting overwhelmed by any adversities, try to understand the difference between being rigid and being dogmatic. Managing and delegating are two important aspects of life but micromanaging merely drains your energy.

So, don't be surprised if you come across events where you need to determine the difference between a responsible and irresponsible course of action. Similarly, it's time to evaluate any self-defeating thoughts or behaviors based on inherent feelings of restriction. Examine the different ways you can shift, change and mold your life to attain professional and personal goals.

Maturity Number 5

Maturity number 5 means you are evaluating what it means to work with independence and freedom. Now is the moment to think about how you can constructively use freedom, add flexibility to your life, cope with uncertainties and embrace the concept of progressive change. The most common challenges faced by this number include the ones caused due to inherent conflicts about discipline and the use of freedom. It is okay to crave freedom and embrace uncertainties of life, but self-discipline is important to attain your goals and ideals.

Don't be surprised if a dramatic change comes up in your life, and it makes you evaluate your sense of freedom. From your child leaving home to divorce or a death in the family, such events can make you question the idea of freedom. It also gives you a chance to think about how you can get what you want from life. If you cannot control your excessive indulgence, especially when it comes to alcohol, food, sex, or drugs, it will become problematic and result in unproductive activities.

Maturity Number 6

It helps you understand what it means to work toward helping others and your family. You have a sense of duty to be of service to others. This number calls upon this inherent sense. You tend to live your life through compassion and affection. The most common challenges associated with this maturity number are associated with modulating responsibility. Sometimes, you might engage in meddling behaviors, display self-righteousness and test the strength of your intimate relationships. These issues can also crop up while you are trying to provide compassionate service to others.

This maturity number is associated with freedom, especially financial freedom that comes via an inheritance or marriage that lets you live the comfortable life you desire. It is a great time to concentrate on your personal life, especially home and family matters. Allow your artistic creativity to concentrate on being of service to others.

Maturity Number 7

Living your life using introspection and spiritual contemplation is what this maturity number is about. You want to understand your true self acts as a homing beacon, showing you the way. The most common challenge you need to deal with is associated with seeking the truth. Sometimes, you need to isolate yourself from others to understand what you desire. You can turn toward research and writing to find spiritual enlightenment and inner peace you so desire.

This maturity number manifestation is characterized by a personal crisis that makes you reevaluate your core beliefs. Your need for solitude and self-introspection make you value the concept of personal space.

Maturity Number 8

This maturity number suggests that you are trying to understand what it means to enjoy the rewards you get through accomplishments. It encourages you to make the most of your talents, coupled with your managerial and organizing abilities to fulfill your achievements. If you use your authority wisely, you can achieve the success and recognition you desire. This number often accompanies a shift in life that brings forth issues associated with achievements in the physical world. Sometimes, you need to step up into the role of a leader and direct others. It's not just about accepting financial abundance and wealth but working for the benefit of society too. It's not always about personal games in life.

If you want to make the most of the guidance offered by this maturity number, look for opportunities that use your managerial, leadership and organizing abilities. This maturity number may bring with it a significant change in your chosen vocation or career. You might also find a new motivation to concentrate more on your professional life to build a career or focus on work instead of concentrating solely on personal relationships, so it's important to maintain the perfect balance between personal and professional lives to make the most of the guidance offered by this number.

Maturity Number 9

The maturity number 9 is all about learning to be of service to others without expecting anything in return. It encourages you to work toward giving and contributing to the general good of society expecting no personal rewards. It helps let go of yourself and think beyond your own needs and desires. It teaches you to let go of particular outcomes while concentrating on tasks. A primary issue you need to watch out for which comes with this number is it can be slightly challenging to balance others' needs with your own. It is okay to be of selfless service, but it is not okay to ignore yourself and your life. Contact your inner philanthropist and teacher without burning yourself out. Understand that self-care is as important as being of service to others.

Master Maturity Number 11

All master numbers bring with them a sense of spiritual purpose. This understanding is true for maturity number 11 too. This maturity number essentially suggests you are on a conscious path toward understanding what it means to harness your emotional sensitivity to help yourself and others. You are also pushed to use your diplomacy and get involved with group dynamics while keeping yourself open to relationships. You are essentially an introverted extrovert and are working toward fame and leadership. The common issues associated with this maturity number can challenge your creativity, sensitivity and the ability to overcome obstacles. The challenges you face are associated with the intensity with which you live life.

Master Maturity Number 22

This master maturity number prompts you to reevaluate what it means to manifest your dreams into reality on a grand scale. It calls out to your inner leader and manager to come to the forefront. Guided by spiritual principles and armed with practical know-how, you can achieve your goals and help others to lead better lives. One area you need to pay attention to will be communication. It's okay to be opinionated but coming across as a know-it-all is undesirable. Temper your bluntness and don't be too rigid in your approach to life. Try to think outside your box, strike a balance between self-care and hard work, to overcome any limitations that may result from your actions.

Chapter 5: Daily Cycles and Patterns

Understanding Daily Cycles

A great thing about numerology is you can use numbers to identify patterns and make daily forecasts about what you can expect every day. By now, you will have realized how important they are. From your birthday to your full name, everything can be simplified to single digits. These numerical equivalents help us obtain some insight into what life has in store. Everything comes in cycles. Everywhere you look, there are numbers, cycles and patterns. All you need is the right information to make the most cues you see in your life.

Unless it is a master number, every significant number of your life can be reduced to a single digit. You don't need your birth year to calculate the daily number. The important numbers you need to do this calculation are your birth month, birth day, current day, current month and the current year. For instance, if you want to know your daily number for December 25, 2020, and your birthday is 30th July, this is how you calculate your daily number.

Since your birth month is 7, the number is 7. Now add the day of your birth, and you end up with 3. Since December is the 12th month of the year, the number is reduced to 3. The desired daily number you are checking for is the 25th of December, which is 7. The desired daily number year in question is 2020, which gives you 4. Now, it's time to add all the single-digit numbers. In this case, it will be 7 + 3 + 3 + 7 + 4, which is 24. So, your desired daily number for 25th December 2020 is 6. Now, let's look at what each of the numbers signifies on any given day.

The interpretations for different numbers are based on the vibrations given by each of them in numerology. It essentially shows the subtle energy or attraction that will flow into your life during a day due to a specific number.

Personal Day Number 1

This number brings with it an energy good for planning new projects or starting new ventures. Is all about self-determination and self-sufficiency. If you are thinking about joining the gym, eating healthy or doing any new activity, today is the day to get started. The subtle energy that resonates with number one helps you get started and do things on your own without worrying about approval.

Personal Day Number 2

By now, you will have realized there is a pattern that each number follows. Their primary traits always stay the same. The energy associated with number 2 resonates with working in groups. It is a great day to work with a team. It allows you to be considerate of other people's feelings and give you the energy to defuse situations with diplomacy and tact. On this day, concentrate on your relationships, and it will be worth your while.

Personal Day Number 3

Number 3 brings with it a lot of creative energy, which will help your self-expression. An ideal outlet for all your creative expression is through social interaction. This energy is filled with optimism that makes life seem better and gives you the strength to tackle any problems that happen in your life. If you need to meet others, attend important meetings, or just interact, number 3 will give you the required energy.

Personal Day Number 4

The energy which resonates with number 4 is organization. Its methodical energy helps you understand that the best way to complete tasks at hand is by doing them the way they were completed before. This consideration helps you think about securing a stable foundation for your future.

Personal Day Number 5

Personal freedom is what number 5 is associated with. Today's energy gives you the inner desire to express yourself and test your personal liberties. Take this opportunity to engage in different activities that seem to inspire you. It becomes easier to look at life from multiple perspectives without getting bogged down by your single perspective.

Personal Day Number 6

Your life's primary areas that resonate with the energy given out by number 6 are your family and home. This gives you a chance to nurture and support all your loved ones. Not just your loved ones, but this energy can also do good for society in general. It makes you compassionate, giving and nurturing. If there is a specific social cause or an idea that appeals to you, work on it today.

Personal Day Number 7

We often ponder about different questions that concern our existence. What is of purpose on this earth? What are our goals? What do we desire? And so on. Number seven's energy encourages self-introspection. It helps you understand that the answers you are seeking will not come from an external source but are present within. Whether it is science or spirituality, this is a great day to accumulate knowledge and wisdom. Trust your intuition to guide the way and work on solving the mysteries within.

Personal Day Number 8

Finance is one aspect of life; most of us struggle with it. Dealing with any form of financial stress can induce great levels of anxiety. Whether it is planning for a secure future, thinking about your savings or investment, or clearing debt, today's the day for this. Accumulating, managing and maintaining materialistic possessions and finances requires patience and an ability to think about the future. These two things become easier when the energy of number 8 is on your side.

Personal Day Number 9

The energy that resonates with personal day number 9 makes you think about society's welfare and the world in general. It will inspire and motivate you to think about how you can contribute to others and not just yourself. Use this day to be of service to others. Think about how you fit into the bigger picture.

Personal Day Master Number 11

The personal energy that resonates with master number 11 is steeped in spirituality. Intuition, peace and harmony are the main ingredients radiated by this number. Today is a great day to focus on anything associated with spirituality. Whether it is your relationships or avenues that help you step into the role of a teacher, indulge in them. The energy of 11 includes all the good vibrations associated with personal day number 2.

Personal Day Master Number 22

The subtle energy vibrations of number 22 give you the strength to manifest your ideas or thoughts into reality for spiritual and social benefit. You will feel organized, practical and filled with a renewed sense of self-confidence, making it easier to work with others. Work with others and use the cooperative energy of 22 to achieve a shared goal. This number also includes the positive energy associated with personal day number 4.

By extending the different energies associated with the personal day numbers, you can gain insight into what lies in store for you every day. Stop wondering, "What will happen tomorrow?" Or "Why do things happen the way they do?" And calculate your personal day numbers. With the power of numerology, it becomes easier to obtain an overview of the potential each day offers.

Understanding and Interpreting the Numerical Patterns

Since numerology is all about numbers, seeing patterns in them is common. If you stumble upon repeated patterns, it is believed to be a sign from the cosmos or the universe. Seeing certain number sequences repeatedly is a message that your energy vibrations are synchronized with the universe, and you are receiving guidance or support from your spirit guides. Since every number has a unique vibration, you can determine the message your spirit guide of the universe is trying to communicate with you based on the sequences you see. Common sequences are 111, 222 and so on. Seeing three numbers in a row such as 333, 444, 111, and so on is a powerful sign from the universe. So, heed this intuitive message by deciphering the meaning of each number. Here is a brief overview of what each number means in numerology and the significance of patterns.

- Number 1 is associated with independence, originality and leadership traits. The appearance of this usually signifies the start of something new.

- Number 2 is about the association, cooperation and sensitivity. This number's appearance is a sign you need to be more cooperative and work with others to achieve your goals.

- Number 3 is associated with self-expression, creativity and a desire for spirituality. The universe is sending you a message about different opportunities available to you based on your creativity.

- Career, stability and professional relationships are denoted by number 4. Seeing this repeatedly can be a warning about a situation associated with your professional life.

- Number 5 brings with it a sense of higher consciousness, adventure and excitement. If you repeatedly see this, it is a sign that good things are in store for you.

- Number 6 is associated with your personal life and family in general. Repeatedly seeing patterns with 6 means you need to concentrate more on your familial ties and responsibilities.

- Number 7 expresses a desire for alignment with your spiritual side. It essentially conveys the message that some opportunities help synchronize your inner self with the cosmos.

- Abundance and prosperity are associated with number 8. If you constantly see patterns with this, it is a sign the universe is sending you guidance to attract abundance and material wealth into your life.

- Number 9 brings with it a deep sense of accomplishment that feeds your soul. If you repeatedly see these patterns, it is a message you need to start concentrating on your life's real purpose.

- Number 11 is a master number that conveys the message; it is time to listen to your intuition and let it guide the way. It can also be a sign you are about to meet someone whose energy vibrations will help increase yours.

- Number 22 is the master builder which is a sign from the universe you have what it takes to manifest your dreams, thoughts and ideas into reality.

The guidance from your spirit guides or the universe often presents itself as a sequence of numbers. Use the information given until now to understand the message the cosmos is trying to communicate. Patterns can come in sets of twos, threes or even fours. For instance, you might see 11, 111 or 1111. What is the difference among these three? The number of ones that appear correspond with the strength and power of the message sent by the universe. If you repeatedly see 111, it means your intuition is at its peak, and it is an opportunity to share your gifts or creativity with others, perhaps through teaching or accepting a leadership role. It can also be a sign it is time to start something new.

222 carries forth the energy of unconditional love and acceptance. If you repeatedly see this pattern, it means now is the time to understand, accept and act on your heart's desires and express yourself clearly. It is also a gentle reminder for you to open yourself up to others and work on forgiveness.

The energy vibrations of 333 are associated with emotion and creation. Seeing this pattern means your body and soul are working in tandem to create and manifest your desires. It is the perfect time to open yourself up to the world and express yourself effectively to tap into your potential.

The energy vibrations of 444 are associated with dreams and hopes. Believe that you can achieve anything and are on the right path toward attaining your goals when you repeatedly see this number pattern. Lay down the foundations for your greatest dreams and believe in yourself that you can see things through. It also suggests financial abundance will soon enter your life.

Change is an important part of life, and unless you learn to let go, you cannot move on. If you repeatedly see number patterns of 555, it means the universe is telling you to let go of everything that doesn't serve your purposes. Accept and be open to change in life because new opportunities will soon present themselves. Once you let go of unnecessary burdens, it becomes easier to move ahead. Think of it as decluttering your body, mind and soul.

Ego and fear are associated with the vibrations of 666. If you see this pattern, the universe is conveying the message that your focus has shifted away from the abundance it offers. All the good is instead replaced by fear and a sense of lacking. You don't have to fear this number even though it is often associated with a negative connotation. This pattern is usually a reminder you need to let go of your fears and accept the bright light of the universe.

The number pattern 777 is associated with your feelings and intuition. If you see this pattern, rest easy knowing you are on the right track, and the universe is helping you along. Follow your intuition, trust your gut, and don't worry if there isn't any factual evidence supporting your intuition. Now is the time to meditate, understand yourself better, and go with your gut.

Growth and transformation are the energies resonating from pattern 888. When you see this pattern, it's a message you have gone through a cycle of change and have transformed. Your strength might have been tested recently, but it's a beautiful reminder you are about to receive bountiful rewards.

999 gives out energy vibrations, which bring about a sense of clarity. If your thoughts are cluttered, and you're feeling scared or overwhelmed, this pattern means you need some mental clarity. Now is the time to start afresh and let go of anything that doesn't add value to your life. Meditation and visualization are two tools to do this.

By understanding the meaning of these number codes and deciphering them, you can increase your self-awareness and grow in life. The next time you instinctively feel different groups of numbers, use the information in this chapter to understand whether its energy matches what you feel.

Chapter 6: The Nine-Year Cycle

In numerology, it is believed that every individual goes through nine-year cycles repeatedly. As soon as one nine-year cycle ends, another begins. It consists of nine cycles wherein each cycle lasts for a year, and each year represents something specific. By understanding the nine-year cycle, you get a better insight into what's in store for you. Discovering where you currently stand in a specific cycle helps sneak a peek into what the future holds. To do this, you need to calculate the universal number and your personal year number.

A basic principle of numerology is that all numbers have specific vibrations. Similarly, every year has underlying energy in sync with its corresponding numbers. This subtle energy cannot be overlooked because it affects everyone who lives on this planet. For instance, the universal year number of 2020 is obtained by adding all the individual numbers in it. So, the universal year number is 2+0+2+0, which is 4.

The year 2020 carries with it the stability, manifesting capacities and practicality associated with the energy of 4. In the previous chapters, you were introduced to the simple steps for calculating your life path number. Because of our different life path numbers, how we experience the universal year number varies. You need to consider the effect of the combined vibrations from both the numbers. To get a better insight into this, you need to calculate your personal year number.

Calculate Your Personal Year Number

Calculating your personal year number is simple. As with the life path number, you need your birth date once again to calculate this number. Instead of your birth year, you need to replace it with the universal year to find your personal year number. So, it is the addition of the individual numbers present in your birth month, birthday and the universal year. Here's a simple example to get a better understanding of how to calculate the personal year number. Let's assume that an individual's birth date is 30th February 1980. Now, it is time to calculate the combined total of the birthday and month.

Personal year number = Birthday + birth month + universal year number

The personal year number in the above example is 30+02+2020, which is 3+2+4= 9. If your personal year is 9, it means you are in the final year of a 9-year cycle.

Deciphering the Nine-Year Cycle

Let's delve a little deeper to understand what each of these years truly represents. It will help better show you what the upcoming year will be like. The nine stages of the cycle are beginning, connecting, creating, building, changing, nurturing, re-evaluating, expanding and competing. Once you go through these nine stages, the cycle starts again. In life, every bit of additional information you can get your hands on will be helpful.

The First Year

This is the first year of the starting of a new nine-year cycle. It brings with it a sense of adventure and a promise of something new. It is the starting point of the next cycle of nine years in your life, which comes with its own set of opportunities and challenges. Before you think about acting on your goals, the first step is to clarify them. Now is the time to do this. Hard work is important to move ahead in life, but it is equally important to have a sense of direction and purpose. Since it is the sign of a new beginning, your energy levels will be higher, and you will feel more motivated than you have for a while. You cannot start afresh unless you make some changes. If you cannot make these changes or aren't able to make them, your opportunities might be delayed until the next cycle starts, and you are willing to make the required change. This is one reason why the beginning of the cycle feels like you are about to set on an incredible adventure.

If there is a specific move for a change you have been thinking of making, now is the time to do it. Perhaps you want to start a family, settle down or shift your job. Whatever it is, now is the time to put your plans into action. Set new goals for yourself and start working towards them. It is best you don't think about your past right now and concentrate only on the future. The beginning of the cycle means the previous cycle has ended. The end of the cycle signifies that your problems and disappointments were solved. In their place, new opportunities await you. Be curious and excited for all that life has in store for you this year.

The Second Year

The second year of the cycle might make you feel as if all you are doing is merely waiting in the background. Don't be surprised if you often find yourself in the background; it is a sign of development. Don't concentrate on forcing yourself to move forward but, instead, shift your focus toward personal development. This is a great time to build relationships that will offer benefits and future. It is all about collection and accumulation. During this year, remember there is no scope for aggression. Aggression will become a cause of different problems in life. Waiting in the background takes a lot of patience.

Don't be disheartened if all you do is make small contributions or offer help. Everything that comes your way is an opportunity for growth and development. Don't think of it as anything other than this.

It also puts your self-control and emotional sensitivities to the test. Concentrate on improving your skills and abilities to work productively with others. If you are used to working independently or have a lone wolf mentality, this will not be easy. Whatever you do, don't give up on your internal sense of peace and calm. Any nervous tension you experience during this year is temporary, and it will go away. Your emotional sensitivities will be extreme, so this is a great time for you to concentrate on your personal relationships.

The Third Year

The third year of the cycle exudes an energy that's bright, joyous and cheerful. It is an incredibly happy and a social year for you. It not only helps you reconnect with your old friends but also broadens your existing social circle. Besides your social circle, your love life will also blossom. The inclination to live your life to the fullest is at its peak. Well, it would be wise if you slowed down and understood there will be consequences to pay later if you aren't careful. The battle of responsibility seems to have diminished this year, and you will be at your sociable best. Your energy might be a little scattered, and there may be too many commitments to cater to.

This year gives you a chance to enjoy yourself, take a break from the stresses of life and have a good time. It is okay to give in to this temptation to have a good time, but don't forget your goals. This is a great year to work on your creative talents, especially the ones associated with art and verbal skills. Don't get disheartened if the recognition you think you deserve doesn't come easily to you this year. For personal expression and activities, this is a wonderful year, but it doesn't carry the same positivity with your professional life. Unfinished business, rash decisions and a carefree attitude will spell disaster for your career, so concentrate on exercising sufficient self-control. Don't lose sight of your goals because of all the distractions this year brings.

The Fourth Year

The fourth year helps you forget about the frivolity the third you brought into your life. If the previous year wasn't good for your finances, you could compensate for its harmful effects this year. If there is a specific task you need to complete, this year gives you the internal design motivation required to put in the hard work and effort to complete it. It also helps reestablish your self-control instead of getting carried away by the distractions of life. In some ways, it can be a little frustrating when all your hard work doesn't produce the dramatic results you hoped for. It may seem as if you're taking one step forward and two steps back usually. Instead of worrying about the results, concentrate on organizing yourself better. It helps you look at your past and present performance to analyze all that you have achieved. By getting organized, it becomes easier to understand the direction in which you are headed.

The Fifth Year

The fifth year of the cycle brings major life changes. These are to help you to expand your horizon and experience growth. Your set of friends will increase, you will indulge more in social activities and you'll meet a lot of new people. This year brings with it a sense of excitement and adventure. You will also experience more freedom than you did in the previous years. It is time to let go and run free. It gives you the courage required to move away from old routines constructively and work on productivity. If you have been feeling restricted until now, this will help you to seek new directions in life. The only problem with this is your energy might be scattered in different directions. Anything that makes you feel confined will lose its appeal quite quickly.

The Sixth Year

This year is all about home, family, love and responsibility. It is an incredibly personal year where your responsibility might increase. On the plus side, it also deepens the bond you share with your loved ones, whether they are your friends or family members. You might need to make some adjustments in your life or sacrifice a few things for your loved ones. It's more about handling and planning adjustments as you find necessary instead of looking for major compliments. Complete all the projects you might have started in the previous years. You may feel as if you are moving slowly, and you aren't able to see any progress, but on a personal front, matters will improve significantly. Accept living life at a slower pace, and you will enjoy the harmony, love and happiness this year brings.

The Seventh Year

The seventh year encourages self-introspection. It is a perfect time to understand yourself and your desires. So, take a break and reflect on your life. Self-contemplation and introspection give you a chance to break free of all the stresses of daily life and understand yourself. This might not be a year of action, but all the waiting and development you experience will make it worthwhile. Studying, writing and working on integrating your thoughts are some of the best activities suitable for this year. You might seem detached and even aloof but it merely means you are focused on yourself. Use this time and effort to hone and master your skills.

The Eighth Year

After all the self-introspection brought in by the previous year, now it's time to make important changes to your life. The storing of ambition can be felt right now. It's time to make major decisions, work toward bigger achievements. Taking action is what it is all about. After all the self-introspection, it becomes easier to understand the path you should be on and the different changes you need to make to attend goals. Things start going easy for you as long as you recognize opportunities for advancement. Self-confidence and authority are the primary energies associated with the eighth year. Whether it is in your personal or professional life, it's time to pull out all stops and work on your dreams. During this year of your personal cycle, your status and power potential are at their peak. Make the most of it by channeling your inner leader.

The Ninth Year

The end is where we start from, and usually, what we call the beginning in life, is often the end. The ninth year completes a nine-year cycle of your life. It is the year to tie up all the loose ends and reach some conclusions. If there is any unfinished business, there is no time like the present to get on with it. Once you tie up all the loose ends, you can move onto the next nine years of your life without the stress of unresolved matters weighing you down. Remember, whenever a door closes, another one opens. You cannot recognize the new possibilities available in your life if you fail to acknowledge that certain doors are meant to be closed and have been closed.

This year is about facing the reality of your past and how it affects your present right through to the desired course of action needed to create the future you desire. The reality is not just about where you are today or where you wish to be tomorrow. Instead, it's the culmination of everything that happened to you, everyone you have met in life, every feeling you've experienced or denied, and every action or inaction of yours. Who you are today results from your past and everything you have experienced. If there is any aspect of your persona that no longer serves a purpose and merely restricts you to a specific period in time that no longer exists, it's time to let go. Since this year is about completion, complete all your businesses, close all the doors and move on.

You can wake nothing in your life unless necessary endings have taken place. This is the year for reaching out and reflection. You might end up scrutinizing your ideals, ideas and values you may have believed were important in life. Learn to become more involved with others during this year instead of just looking out for yourself.

Chapter 7: The Life Cycle

The journey you want to take in life can be divided into three portions of time known as the major life cycles. These stages represent how you grow and progress in life. The three life cycles are youth, maturity and wisdom. Every major life cycle number comes with its own set of characteristics and traits that will help you grow. The three major life cycles are the areas of development that help fulfill your destiny as you progress through life. Throughout a life cycle, you will learn about the different opportunities and challenges that will come up during your life.

So, how can you calculate your major life cycle number? Well, you just need your birth date for this purpose. The first step is to reduce the corresponding numbers of your birth month, day and year down to three single-digit individual numbers unless they are master numbers. If you have the numbers 11 or 22 as the month, year or day of birth, don't reduce them to 2 or 4. Here is a simple example to get a better understanding of how this number is calculated. Let us calculate the major life cycle numbers for the birth date 11 December 1996. The single-digit numbers or the numbers for your birth date are 11, 12 and 7.

The first major life cycle number is known as your youth number.

The second major life cycle number is the cycle of maturity number and this is your month of birth, the maturity number is your day of birth, and the wisdom number is your year of birth.

The third major life cycle number is the cycle of wisdom, the cycle of youth and the cycle of youth numbers.

In the example mentioned above, with the date of birth 11/12/1996 (DD/MM/YYYY format), the major life cycle numbers are as follows.

The first major life cycle number = 3

The second major life cycle number = 11

The third major life cycle number = 7

Let us look at the different age groups through which different life path numbers progress.

Life Path Number 1

- First cycle age- 0- 26 years
- Second cycle age- 27-53 years
- Third cycle age- 54 years and upward

Life Path Number 2

- First cycle age- 0- 25 years
- Second cycle age- 26-52 years
- Third cycle age- 53 years and upward

Life Path Number 3

- First cycle age- 0- 33 years
- Second cycle age- 34-60 years
- Third cycle age- 61 years and upward

Life Path Number 4
- First cycle age- 0-32 years
- Second cycle age- 33-59 years
- Third cycle age- 60 years and upward

Life Path Number 5
- First cycle age- 0-31 years
- Second cycle age- 32-58 years
- Third cycle age- 59 years and upward

Life Path Number 6
- First cycle age- 0-30 years
- Second cycle age- 31-57 years
- Third cycle age- 58 years and upward

Life Path Number 7
- First cycle age- 0-29 years
- Second cycle age- 30-56 years
- Third cycle age- 57 years upward

Life Path Number 8
- First cycle age- 0-28 years
- Second cycle age- 29-55 years
- Third cycle age- 56 years and upward

Life Path Number 9
- First cycle age- 0-27 years
- Second cycle age- 28-54 years
- Third cycle age- 55 years and upward

Life Path Number 11

- First cycle age- 0-26 years
- Second cycle age- 27-53 years
- Third cycle age- 54 and upwards

Life Path Number 22

- First cycle age- 0-32 years
- Second cycle age- 33-59 years
- Third cycle age- 60 years and upward

So, what do each of these life cycle numbers signify for you?

Major Life Cycle Number 1

If your major life cycle number is one, you lean toward independence and love to stand on your own two feet. It gives you a chance to channel your inner leader. This number helps you to walk the path of your choosing and the confidence of trusting your decisions. Throughout your life, the energy vibrations given out by this number make you internally strong, courageous and filled with incredible self-confidence.

You are not bothered by what others think or believe because you know it is not your responsibility to make others happy. You don't have to change yourself because of what others believe, and you understand this truth. This number is a great cycle to start a new venture. Whether it is your personal or professional life, if there is something you want to do, start immediately. From self-employment to starting a business or stepping into a managerial role and advancing your career, this number represents new beginnings.

Major Life Cycle Number 2

The major life cycle number 2 encourages corporation, compassion and sensitivity toward oneself and others. It helps you solve issues diplomatically and learn to make compromises to bring about a sense of harmony to the world. During this, you will be tempted to explore your spiritual and emotional sides to rebalance your life. The universe is now allowing you to tap into your psychic abilities and intuition. This is an ideal time to enter a partnership, stay in a committed relationship, settle down and serve society.

Major Life Cycle Number 3

The major life cycle number 3 gives you a chance to explore your creativity and imagination. This is a period for incredible self-expression. Whether you are expressing yourself artistically, verbally, emotionally or even physically, this year teaches you positive ways of doing this instead of repressing your inner self. You become adept at communicating effectively and efficiently while turning to your creative inclinations. Whether you want to pick up a new hobby, read, paint or draw, write a book or turn to any other artistic avenues, now is the right time.

Major Life Cycle Number 4

The major life cycle number 4 is about working hard and laying down the framework for the future you desire. You value the importance of discipline, dedication, and formal organization while creating something for yourself. It teaches you to persevere, become resilient and overcome any obstacles that come your way while you work on your goals. This is the ideal time to concentrate on your career, renovate your home, commit to a relationship and work on your finances.

Major Life Cycle Number 5

The major life cycle number 5 makes you adaptable and flexible. Number 5 teaches you to value freedom and the need for moderation in all aspects of your life. The desire to explore new places, meet new people, and indulge in new experiences will become your priority during this period. However, while you are busy with all this, don't forget about the bigger picture in life. It is the right time to travel, learn something new, work on self-development and make any significant life changes.

Major Life Cycle Number 6

This number teaches you to take personal responsibility, especially toward your career and relationships with loved ones. You have an inherent desire to be helpful to others and prioritize their needs over your own. During this period, you will learn personal lessons about the importance of love and relationships in life. You also discover the importance of personal boundaries. You finally strike the right balance between playing the roles of a giver and receiver. It is the ideal time to get married, start a family, commit to your relationships, and look for a profession that is service-oriented.

Major Life Cycle Number 7

During this life cycle, you have a desire to peek behind the façade of superficiality. You look for deeper meanings of your desires and are in search of meaningful relationships and things in life. Personal development and delving into your spirituality are the two defining characteristics of this major life cycle. This is the ideal time to focus on yourself and your chosen career. It helps you to be at peace with yourself, and you understand that being alone differs from being lonely. This is the ideal time to improve yourself, develop your intervention, concentrate on your spirituality, and study.

Major Life Cycle Number 8

The major life cycle number 8 encourages you to rethink any undesirable notions about life and finances. Your experience and inherent desire to step into the role of a leader will help progress in your chosen field. You find it easy to stand up for yourself and love taking charge of situations. As long as you put in the required effort and are dedicated to the cause, maintaining healthy relationships in life becomes easier. You attract abundance in all aspects of life. It is the right time to start a business, explore self-employment opportunities, step into the role of a leader, make great strides in your career, and deal with any legal or financial matters.

Major Life Cycle Number 9

This major life cycle number teaches you to understand, accommodate and be compassionate toward yourself and others. It brings with it a broad-mindedness that helps you connect with people from all aspects of life. Forgiving and forgetting is the true representation of this major life cycle. You concentrate on healing yourself and forgiving others for any hurt or grievance they caused in the past. It is the right time to take up a humanitarian cause, serve the community, work on your artistic talents, let go of past trauma and improve relationships with your loved ones.

Major Life Cycle Number 11

This major life cycle number gives you the energy required to increase your consciousness and work on personal development. This is a period of personal growth. As you work on improving and transforming yourself to be your better version, you can pass on this knowledge to others. You finally find inner peace and use it to inspire others. It is the right time to study any form of healing, psychology to counseling, look for a service-oriented profession and work on developing your intuition and spiritual awareness.

Major Life Cycle Number 22

The major life cycle number 22 prompts you to do something that helps others and not just you. Think about where you fit in the bigger picture of life and how you can help others. You want to be of service to the community, your loved ones and the world in general. You might initiate or be engaged in any form of work or service that helps bridge the gap between the real and spiritual realms.

Chapter 8: Charts and Arrows

By now, you have realized numerology is incredibly simple. There's nothing complicated about it. All you need are certain simple calculations, and you can use it to determine your strengths and weaknesses, understand what life has in store and make the most of all the opportunities which come your way. If you are interested in learning more about your numerological chart, let's get started.

The first step toward understanding your numerological chart is through the arrows of Pythagoras. This is a simple and fun way to understand your weaknesses and course trends represented by your date of birth. Every numerological charge doesn't necessarily have arrows. If there are no arrows in your chart, it isn't a bad thing. It's merely a representation of your flexible personality. It means you can easily get accustomed to changing circumstances in life. To draw a numerological chart and find arrows of Pythagoras, the first step is to create a 3 x 3 grid, which will look like this.

In this grid, write down the numbers from 1-9 as follows:

3	6	9
2	5	8
1	4	7

Now, you need to place each number of your birth date in its appropriate square, which was discussed above. If there are any zeros in your birth date, leave them out. For instance, if your birth date is 07.07.1970, the grid will look like this:

		9
11		77

To draw a Pythagoras arrow, you need to join three squares that contain numbers or the ones that have no numbers. The arrows can be drawn horizontally, vertically or diagonally. If there are no numbers present in a row, whether it is diagonally, horizontally or vertically, it is known as an empty arrow. In the previous example, the numbers 2, 5, 8, and 4, 5, 6 are absent. 2, 5 8 is the arrow of emotion, and 4, 5, 6 are the arrow of frustration. You will learn more about what the presence or absence of these arrows means later in this chapter. For now, let's look at another example. Let's consider the birthdate 25. 09. 1980. Fill out the corresponding grids with the numbers of this birthdate. When you do this, the grid will look like this.

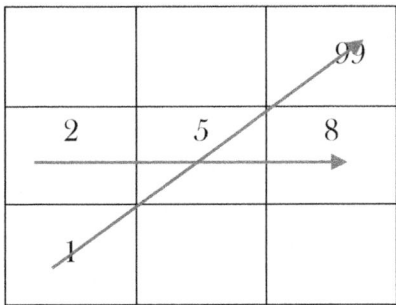

The grids that can be joined are the ones wherein three numbers are present. There are two full arrows in this example- 2, 5, 8, and 1, 5, and 9.

Are you wondering what a full and empty arrow means? In numerology, a full arrow represents positive traits or strengths, and an empty arrow represents weaknesses. Positive traits or strengths are your natural skills that can be utilized and improved upon to enhance your life's overall quality. An empty arrow shows areas where you are lacking and tend to identify with negative patterns. Understanding all this information makes it easier to take the required action to make the most of what life has to offer.

Meanings of Full Arrows

Arrow of Planning - 1, 2, 3

A full arrow 1, 2, 3 means you are an excellent planner, or your mind is constantly busy thinking about every little detail, is analyzing, and organizing all the information it absorbs and has retained. It is a true representation of your independent personality and your love for personal freedom and independence of thought. These are strengths in your professional life but can become significant obstacles in your relationships. This arrow in an intimate relationship might make you seem aloof, selfish and detached.

Arrow of Willpower - 4, 5, 6

This full arrow in your chart is a representation of your incredible determination and inherent self-control. Whether it is responsibilities, challenges, big projects or anything else that life throws at you, you will be triumphant. You are individualistic and learned to be self-reliant at an early age. Due to this, you might seem a little stubborn in your personal relationships. To ensure that your personal energy level stays well balanced, don't overexert yourself.

Arrow of Activity - 7, 8, 9

If the full arrow of activity is present in your numerology chart, it means physical activity is a significant part of your life. A job that keeps you on your feet and constantly includes some form of movement or other will be ideal for you. You are extroverted and love to interact with others whether or not it's your loved ones or strangers. Since you love to be on the move all the time, taking a break and relaxing might seem difficult for you. Therefore, take a moment, step back and enjoy all that life hasn't supplied for you. If you don't take care of yourself, you will be exhausted, which will cause unnecessary agitation and boredom.

Arrow of Determination - 1, 5, 9

You are a true "go-getter" if the arrow of determination is present in your numerology chart. Some traits you are blessed with are your ambition, patience and persistence. Your desire for these things makes you play well with rigid rules. For working toward your goals and attaining them, you are focused. You don't easily get distracted and have a fine-tuned focus that brings you closer to your goals. This can make you a little rigid and inflexible. Since change is the only constant in life, you need to learn to be more adaptable. It becomes easier to succeed and bring about a sense of harmony to all aspects of your life if you learn to listen to different opinions and become flexible.

Arrow of Practicality - 1, 4, 7

If the arrow of practicality is present in your numerical chart, it means you are skilled in the physical realm. You are well-grounded and have a strong sense of reality, which prevents you from getting distracted by the unimportant details in life. However, you may concentrate too much on the material aspects of life and forget about enjoying the little joys life presents.

Arrow of Emotions - 2, 5, 8

As the name suggests, individuals who have a full arrow of emotions are emotionally balanced and intelligent. Emotional balance is important for your overall well-being and happiness in life. Your emotions regulate your thoughts, thoughts regulate your behavior, and behavior regulates the course of your life. Unless you learn to control your emotions, they will control you. Giving in to your emotions can cause rushed and harsh decisions with significant consequences you need to bear. The great thing about this arrow of emotions is it influences your personal energy to be warm and nurturing. It's quite easy for you to connect with others and form meaningful relationships. All the trials and tests that life has thrown at you have strengthened your character. Using these inherent strengths, you can concentrate on sharing your wisdom to help others.

Arrow of Intellect - 3, 6, 9

Intellect and sophistication are two traits common to individuals with a full arrow of intellect. You are not only in tune with your emotions but those of others too. This tendency makes you empathetic. Once you are empathetic, it becomes easier to understand what others feel and why they feel the way they do. Empathy is an important trait in all aspects of your life, whether it is in your personal or professional life. You are focused on your mental and intellectual development. Besides all those key areas of your life, you need to concentrate on your communication and intimacy.

Arrow of Compassion - 3, 5, 7

The arrow of compassion is also known as the arrow of spirituality. Individuals with this arrow are empathetic. The traits you might associate with it are loyalty, creativity, faithfulness and kindness. Concentrate on gaining a sense of inner balance to grow emotionally and spiritually.

Meanings of Empty Arrows

Now, let's look at what you can understand through the presence of empty arrows in your numerology chart. Empty arrows are often believed to be the embodiment of negative traits. Instead, it will do you good to understand these are certain areas of your life where there is some scope for improvement. When you know where you need to improve yourself, it becomes easier to take the desired course of action.

Arrow of Impracticality - 1, 4, 7

You are a dreamer, and this can make you impractical. It is okay to dream, but it is equally important to understand you need to live in the real realm. Introverts and artists tend to have this arrow. You might have wonderful ideas and incredible goals but might not have the energy required to manifest them into reality. This is one area where you are severely lacking. You cannot achieve your dreams and goals if you don't take the desired action to get there. What is the point of having a clear destination in mind if you aren't sure of the route you need to take? Therefore, don't just concentrate on dreaming big, but also create a solid plan of action to get there. Remember, life is riddled with challenges and obstacles, so plan for them too. Once you do all this, it becomes easier to find the manifestation potential within.

Arrow of Frustration - 4, 5, 6

If this empty arrow is present in your Numerological chart, you probably often find yourself quite frustrated. It's not just frustration with yourself, but with others and even the world in general. Everything and anything seems to trigger you. You also might have the attitude of "My way or the highway." This can create plenty of trouble for you along the way if you are not careful. It is okay to stand up for yourself and be confident about what you believe in, but it is equally important to be flexible in life. Learn to stop being critical of yourself and others. Instead, focus all your energies on inculcating a sense of acceptability. Once you accept yourself, others and life, everything becomes simpler. Don't get overwhelmed, but instead, learn to take control by concentrating on acceptability.

Arrow of Hesitation - 7, 8, 9

There are different instances in life when we hesitate. We hesitate when we don't have the full information to make a decision; we hesitate while trying new things or even with experimentation itself. However, if you find yourself constantly hesitating and not taking any action, it boils down to the arrow of hesitation in your numerological chart. It is essentially a representation of low levels of motivation, determination and a sense of purpose. Without these three things, you cannot get anywhere in life. You might also be at a greater risk of idealizing and having unrealistic expectations. Unrealistic expectations increase the likelihood of disappointment. It also increases the chances of giving up. Therefore, learn to be more action-oriented. Unless you take the first step, you will never know. Concentrate on working toward your goals, keeping your goal small, measurable, attainable, realistic and time-bound. One skill you can benefit from is developing self-discipline. It helps you to tackle any hesitation you experience and makes you a go-getter.

Arrow of Poor Memory - 3, 6, 9

The most prominent effect of the arrow of poor memory often shows up during the early ages of an individual's life. From learning difficulties to trouble concentrating, these are all associated with the arrow of poor memory. You might also notice you tend to get bored quite easily and lose track of things. Therefore, concentrate on working to improve your memory and concentration. The good news is you have complete control over these two aspects of your brain. Instead of concentrating on multitasking, focus solely on one task. You can also try meditation to gain but control over your thoughts.

Arrow of Emotional Sensitivity - 2, 5, 8

The arrow of emotional sensitivity discussed in the previous section brings with it emotional stability and balance. The absence of this arrow makes you overly sensitive to emotions and energies. This sensitivity is not just to the emotions and energies of others present around you, but the ones present within two. You feel tired and drained when spending time with others. You have a great sense of intuition and are blessed with psychic abilities that others cannot see. The only way to maintain your emotional sensitivity and balance is by developing a strong sense of inner balance. Once the world within you is well balanced, you can finally regain control of your emotions.

Arrow of Skepticism - 3, 5, 7

Skepticism is important in life because it helps you differentiate between reality and fiction. Skepticism is not always about a thing. However, if you deny information that lies outside your comfort zone or conventional norms you are used to, it becomes obstacle. The arrow of skepticism can make you hyper-vigilant, prone to anxiety and even obsessive at times in personal relationships. Therefore, the one thing you need to concentrate on is opening yourself up to new experiences, alternate concepts, multiple perspectives and your opinions of others.

Arrow of Indecision - 1, 5, 9

The arrow of indecision can be challenging, especially when you cannot decide on what you want to do or where you are heading. How can you ever follow through on your decisions if you're not sure of the decision you've already made? Indecision is paralyzing in life. Even though you have a tough time following through with your decisions, you are good at developing new ideas. Work on improving your self-confidence, and this indecision will slowly go away. Instead of getting overwhelmed thinking about taking big risks or following lofty goals, concentrate on smaller steps. Live your life with the idea of one step at a time.

Chapter 9: Calculating Relationships

A common reason people turn to numerology is that they want to learn about their relationship compatibility. Humans are social creatures, and we cannot survive without relationships. One of the most important bonds you will ever form in life is with your special someone. Whether it is the romantic movies or novels, we have all grown up with finding our other half. With numerology, relationship compatibility is determined by calculating the relationship number.

Don't be under any misconception that the lack of compatibility in numerology means the relationship is doomed. Every relationship requires work, and this is the only thing you need to remember.

The relationship number has a special place in numerology. This is better than comparing the separate numerological chart of both partners in the relationship. A relationship number is a single number that encompasses all that the relationship has to offer. Calculating this is quite simple. It is calculated from the life numbers of both partners.

Calculate the life number; you need to add the life path number and the expression number. Once you do this, the sum needs to be reduced to a single-digit number between 1 and 9 unless it's one of the master numbers 11 or 22. In the previous chapter, you were given all the information you need to calculate both these numbers. Calculate the life path number for yourself and your partner. After this, just add them and reduce them to a single-digit between 1- 9 or leave it as 11 or 22 for master numbers.

Here's a simple example to get a better understanding of how the life numbers are calculated. Let us assume that your life path number is 8, and the expression number is 6. So, your life number will be 5 (6 + 8). If your partner's life path number is 7 and the expression number is 9, their life number will be 7 (7 + 9). The final step is to add your life number to that of your partners. So, you will end up with relationship number 3 (5+7). This number is unique to your relationship. Now let's look at interpreting each of these relationship numbers.

Relationship Number 1

If you and your partner have something to focus on, this relationship will thrive and prosper. Ambitions and goals are key to this relationship. Maybe you have plans to shift to an exotic location, start a family together, build your home or maybe even a business. Both partners in this relationship have incredible skills, and when you put them together, it enhances what you each can achieve individually. You are the ultimate power couple and will inspire others. If you think your relationship is struggling, you probably have both lost your common purpose and are slowly drifting away from each other. Pump more energy into this relationship, and it will prosper again. Think about starting something new together and make sure you are both passionate about it. It will help rekindle the fire, sparks and passion in the relationship. This newfound passion will help build a thriving partnership that pushes you toward a common goal.

Relationship Number 2

Communication is the most important aspect of a relationship defined by number two. It doesn't matter whether you are both expressive as individuals, but it is important for the health of your relationship. You can use each other's support system to develop better communication skills. It also makes it easier to be sensitive and caring toward one another. The purpose of this relationship is not to balance out any qualities or traits you possess as individuals. Instead, it's about looking for your inner sense of balance.

If your relationship is going through a rough patch right now, it will pass. In the meanwhile, you both need to make a conscious effort and create more time and space for one another. Learn to listen and connect with no judgments. Keep an open heart and mind with your partner. Or maybe you have both forgotten what it means to compromise. A relationship is riddled with compromises. A compromise doesn't mean you are giving up on something you love. Instead, it's merely about making certain adjustments for the sake of love and your relationship. The relationship is not about a single individual but instead, it is about both of you. It is a partnership.

Relationship Number 3

Working and creating together is what makes this relationship exciting. Don't restrict your inner child and let it come out sometimes. This relationship needs to be exciting, playful and therefore you both need to be expressive. This is important if you both have other responsibilities and jobs that take away your inner sense of freedom and inhibition. Tune into your carefree nature, and watch your relationship grow. Social settings or any other situations that let you live life to the fullest are the key to a happy and successful relationship influenced by number 3.

If you have lost this element of fun, your relationship can struggle. Therefore, learn to bring in more energy and don't get caught in the mundane routines. Let go of your inhibitions, be spontaneous and permit yourself to be silly.

Relationship Number 4

If you and your partner are concentrating on building a future together, this relationship will be the best thing that's happened to you. Staying grounded and feeling organized are two things quite essential for this relationship. Adding routines and having a general sense of direction will be good for you both. Even if both your life path numbers don't adhere to these conditions, this is what the future of your relationship relies on. Your solid and stable partnership is an inspiration to others, and it is admirable.

If you have both become ungrounded, this relationship will struggle a little. Focus more on the little details of the life you spend together. Delegate responsibilities, share duties, and work out the practicalities of your personal life together. If this firm rooting is absent, your relationship will not survive.

Relationship Number 5

Exploring the wonders of life is what keeps this relationship alive. Every turn of the relationship needs to feel exciting and new. If you and your partner are spontaneous and a little carefree, this partnership will be rewarding. It also means you both need to give each other plenty of personal space while making time for adventures together. Organize your life so you can add some diversity to it while keeping things exciting without forgetting about responsibilities. Don't get caught up in the practicalities of life and forget to smell the roses once in a while. Learn to grow and stay together without compromising on your freedom.

If your life gets mundane, the relationship will become stale. There are different activities you can indulge in to rekindle the energy of five into your relationship. Something as simple as a date night or an impromptu getaway will work wonders. Add a touch of variety, and your relationship will be as good as new again.

Relationship Number 6

In a healthy, lasting and strong relationship, there needs to be a sense of security. You are your partner sanctuary, and vice versa. Unless this element exists in your relationship, it cannot evolve. Therefore, your relationship needs to give out safe and positive energy. In this wonderful space you are both creating together, there's nothing you cannot achieve together. It also gives you a chance to express your creative gifts with no worries, fears or anxiety. The energy given out by you as a couple is something that attracts many people to your house. The party never ends at your house.

If you do not nurture this relationship, it will wither away. Therefore, be careful. It is important to socialize with others, but it is equally important to spend time with each other. If your schedule is getting quite hectic, take a break, and make time and space for each other. After all, how can a relationship survive if both partners are not together? Make it a point it is an equal partnership. One cannot be the receiver and the other the nurturer. Once you attain this equilibrium in the relationship and make sure you are both being cared for, your relationship will become strong. Taking care of each other is simple. Perhaps you can cook your partner's favorite meal, go to their favorite restaurant, or maybe even watch a movie you both love together. It's always about the gestures you make that help the partnership to last and be fulfilling.

Relationship Number 7

Relationship number 7 signifies that the bond between the partners needs to be deep. Superficiality is not a sign of a healthy or lasting relationship. In this relationship, you both need to feel like you are on a quest to find the deeper meaning of life. By working on each other's knowledge and looking for creative and authentic ways to live life, you will try to prosper together as a couple. You both love spending time together with no distractions. This helps explore your lives together and see it is molded according to your desires.

A common challenge this relationship number faces is from an external source. If societal norms and expectations of your loved ones become restrictive or cumbersome, your relationship will struggle. Therefore, it's time to get away from all this. Let go of external expectations and instead concentrate on each other and what you both desire. Sit down and have an open and honest conversation about where you want the relationship to head. When you work together as a team, you will both be inspired to do better individually.

Relationship Number 8

There is a free flow of wealth and power in this relationship. It almost feels as if you're both building an empire together. However, there must always be a balance of power between the partners. If not, the relationship will struggle a little. Number 8 is associated with balance. However, its energy might also represent rising and fall. Therefore, your relationship will go through several stages and cycles. The only thing that matters is you are both in it together and don't let go of each other. These ups and downs are not anyone's fault, and this is the manifestation of the energy associated with the number 8.

The simplest way to rebalance and re-energize your relationship is by addressing any imbalances in your partnership. Don't worry about who is in charge of what. Instead, learn to take responsibility for things together. If not, the responsibilities can be equally divided out. Once you do this, you can both work together as a team to build the empire you desire.

Relationship Number 9

Since relationship number 9 is associated with spirituality, you will both have an inherent desire to be of service to others. At times, the relationship might feel as if it is operating on a higher plane of reality that isn't confined by the restrictions of the physical realm. Whether it does contribute to a charity you are passionate about or offering helpful advice, you will both do it gladly. However, ensure that you have sufficient energy for each other. After all, the relationship is about you and not all the good you do for others. Look at the bigger picture, but it is equally important to look at your relationship. If you are both too caught up and doing your bit for society, this relationship can struggle a little. Instead, shift your focus inwards and toward your relationship. What can you do for each other? What do you bring to the table? How can you help your relationship? These are questions you both need to answer together.

Relationship Number 11

Since master number 11 is deeply rooted in spirituality, if both partners are on a spiritual journey together, the relationship will thrive. As for relationship number 2, you both need to communicate effectively. Besides communication, there needs to be mutual care, empathy and sensitivity. Understand that the purpose of your relationship is not true to balance each other's traits but to gain a sense of inner balance. Once you are both at peace, the relationship will prosper. Being energetic and interested in spiritual awakening comes with its own set of challenges. So, you both need to brace yourselves and get through all the hurdles that come your way because the relationship is truly worth it. The number 11 represents two pillars that stand strong together. You are both equals in the relationship. The wonderful insights, coupled with your deep integration, will be helpful for both of you. Since it is a highly spiritual number, you both need to stay grounded in the physical realm and not get carried away full stock.

Relationship Number 22

This relationship excels when both the partners work together to create a visionary future together. It essentially means you both need to accept your gift and work on creating specific routines. This helps your relationship stay organized and grounded. These are two trades that appeal to both of you. Once you have a solid base, it becomes easy to communicate effectively and efficiently. You can also share your brilliant plans for creating a wonderful future together. Individuals with relationship number 22 have incredible potential to manifest great things that will help this world become a better place.

If there are any issues in your relationship, the only aspect you need to concentrate on is communication. Once you both communicate openly, honestly and from a deeper place, most of your issues will subside. This is a powerful master number, and you should never isolate yourself from each other. Remember, you are both a unit and need to work together. Don't get too carried away with spirituality and take time for yourselves.

Chapter 10: Ayurveda and Numerology

Ayurveda is a Sanskrit term, which translates to "knowledge of life." When people talk about Ayurveda, they think of alternative medicine. Well, Ayurveda is so much more than just medicine. It is a way of life and an healthy one at that. For over 5000 years, the system has been actively used in India. It includes a variety of lifestyle practices such as yoga, dietary changes, meditation, herbal remedies and massages to improve one's overall health and prevent or treat illnesses. This is a holistic medicine that views the body and mind as a single component. Unlike western medicine that tries to look for a universal treatment for a problem, Ayurveda believes every individual is unique. Instead of dealing with only the physical ailments or problems an individual has, Ayurveda improves one's overall health and wellbeing.

Ayurvedic philosophy is based on the universal law of nature about balance. This is one reason why Ayurveda helps balance your external and internal wellbeing.

There are five basic elements - water, earth, fire, air, and space that constantly interact with us and each other form of creation. These elements are categorized into three primary types of energy and principles that apply to everything, and everyone present in this world.

These three components or doshas are known as Vata, Pitta and Kapha. These doshas are not only associated with the primary elements of nature but all our bodily functions too.

Kapha denotes water and earth. It represents our immune system and the physical structure of the human body. Even our emotional responses, such as our ability to love, forgive, and stay calm are governed by Kapha.

Vatta denotes air and space. Our joints, muscles, heartbeat and breathing are all governed by this component of the universe. It is also responsible for governing our nervous system and regulating pain and anxiety.

Pitta denotes fire and water. This element governs important bodily functions such as intelligence, metabolism, digestion and skin color. It is also responsible for governing certain powerful emotions such as hatred and jealousy.

These three doshas are determined at a time of birth and relate to our overall personality and basic physical makeup. For instance, the Kapha body structure is well developed and usually bigger than Vatta's small and thin build or the pitta's medium muscular build. For once overall wellbeing, all these three doshas need to be balanced in your body. Any imbalance in these shows results in illnesses and other conditions which harm our health. Ayurvedic practices are good for maintaining your overall health, improving flexibility, strengthening your body and mind, enhancing your stamina, reducing stress and even tackling other harmful conditions such as arthritis, asthma and high blood pressure.

Did you know there are eight branches in Ayurveda? It includes pediatrics, internal medicine, ear, nose and throat treatment, surgery, psychiatry, toxicology, fertility and conception therapy, geriatrics and rejuvenation. Besides all this, Ayurveda offers a wonderful cleansing protocol termed Panchakarma. It uses five therapies to help your body let go of all the toxins stored within its tissues and muscles while rebalancing doshas. Ayurveda is based on the principle of balance. It's believed everything in the universe has its own specific vibration. This theory is similar to the belief in numerology.

Vedic Numerology

Vedas are ancient Indian texts of knowledge and wisdom on different topics written thousands of years ago. Until now, you were introduced to the concept of western numerology. There is one other branch of numerology, which is vastly studied, and it is Vedic numerology. Vedic numerology uses numbers to study and get a better understanding of human behavior, temperament, natural disposition, destiny, sexuality, intelligence and so on. This form of numerology stems from Samkhya philosophy and Vedic rituals symbolism. Samkhya means numbers, and it forms the basis for Ayurveda and yoga too. It is closely related to the different patterns present in nature, the composition and construction of the human body, and the importance and role of different organs present. It seeks to understand the numbers hidden in objects, living beings and different patterns that somehow shape human personality.

One of the most important differences between Vedic and western numerology is associated with numeral representations. In Vedic numerology, it's believed that every number is associated with specific deities. According to Vedic teachings, deities are the representation of different planets. There are nine numbers in Vedic numerology, and 9 corresponding deities or planets represent them.

Numerology plays an important role in Hinduism, even today. Certain days of the year are considered auspicious, while some are inauspicious. Different numbers bring with them the influence of different planets. Certain rituals and ceremonies such as marriage, naming ceremony of a newborn, starting a business venture, and so on are performed at a specific time on a given day. In Vedic tradition, astronomy and astrology are closely related. There are patterns in everything, and numbers form these patterns. Numbers by themselves hold a special place in Vedic philosophies. For instance, the rosary beads used for repeating mantras have 108 beads. The distance between the sun and the earth is 108 times the Sun's diameter. Therefore, the number 108 is believed to be the key to attaining spiritual enlightenment.

There is as such no importance for zero in numerology. This number by itself has no value. Its placement determines its value. Even though it adds no value to numerological calculations, it holds special significance in numerology. Zero is known as Shoonya in Sanskrit. It is believed to symbolize the beginning and the end. It is the embodiment of nothingness and the void. Everything comes from Shoonya and goes back to Shoonya in the end.

Number 1

It is associated with the sun. Individuals with this number have a strong sense of individuality, masculine energy, they love to be in control and love their personal freedom. They are also intelligent, bright and love all the comforts and luxuries of life.

Number 2

It is associated with the moon. Individuals with this number are emotional, intuitive, gentle, nurturing and peace-loving. Their personalities are flexible and attractive.

Number 3

It is associated with the planet Jupiter. Individuals with this number are energetic, spiritual, disciplined and strongly built. They prefer rational thinking, work on acquiring more knowledge and are dutiful.

Number 4

It is associated with the planet Rahu. Individuals with this number are often stubborn, moody, short-tempered, impulsive and unpredictable. They can also be secretive and selfish to a great extent.

Number 5

It is associated with the planet Mercury. Individuals with this number have a child-like nature playful, free-spirited, adaptable and sensitive. They are also logical, bright and have progressive thinking.

Number 6

It is associated with the planet Venus. Individuals with this number are sensuous, friendly, artistic, soft-spoken and well organized. The gentle nature, coupled with creativity and tact, makes them approachable.

Number 7

It is associated with the planet Ketu. Individuals with this number are insightful, dreamy, indecisive and intuitive. They believe in mysticism, are drawn to religions and are sentimental and highly insightful. They also love nature, and everything associated with it.

Number 8

It is associated with the planet Saturn. Individuals with this number are strong-willed, introverted, thoughtful, caring and protective. They are hardworking, wise and subservient.

Number 9

It is associated with the planet Mars. Individuals ruled by the planet Mars are short-tempered, have a dominating personality, are aggressive, strong and have strong leadership traits. Don't let their harsh exterior fool you because they're quite soft on the inside.

All the different qualities corresponding to the planetary deities must never be taken in that literary sense because they manifest in humans in varying degrees. According to Vedic philosophy, every human being is a unique distinct destiny and karma. Therefore, several factors need to be considered while determining the primary characteristics and traits, along with the destiny of individuals. In Vedic numerology, only the numbers matter. Other factors that are important in astrology, such as planetary positions, don't matter here.

The psychic number or the birth number is calculated based on the birth day. If the number is greater than 9, they need to be reduced to a single digit. The psychic number plays an important role in shaping your overall personality and behavior. It also influences all the choices you make in life, whether about the food you wish to eat or the profession you choose and the goals you set and other personal relationships. Because every number is associated with a planetary deity, the qualities associated with the corresponding deity manifest in individuals born under the specific number.

The destiny number is calculated by summing up all the individual digits present in your full date of birth. So, it is important because it influences the course of your life and destiny too. Your destiny combines your past karma and any latent impressions leftover from your previous birth. This number becomes especially important after the age of 35. By adding the numerological value of all the letters in your birth name, you will arrive at your name number. While doing this, there is a significant difference between western and Vedic numerology. Every alphabet is assigned a value between the numbers one and eight. Number 9 is excluded from calculations present in the Vedic square because adding it to any other number does not alter the number's primary value. For instance, $3 + 9 = 12$ or 3, $2+9 = 11$ or 2, $1+9= 10$ or 1.

You might recall from the previous chapters based on calculations of your full name; western astrology concentrates only on the full birth name, excluding any suffixes. In Vedic astrology, you can calculate the name number for your nicknames and even other aliases. If you are usually referred to by your last name at work, the number will be based on your last name to determine your work life. If you are known by your nickname at home, your home life is determined by the number culminating from the sum of your nickname and so on. The name number per se exudes little influence on your destiny, but it influences your birth number and general behavior in life.

A primary difference between Vedic numerology and western numerology is in the treatment of master numbers such as 11 and 22. In Vedic numerology, this concept does not exist. For instance, if the sum of one's destiny number, life path number, or any other number results in 11 or 22, it is further converted to a single digit that makes it 2 or 4. Everything in Vedic numerology is converted to a single digit. For instance, if the birthdate is 03/06/2000, the life number will be 2(3 + 6 + 2 = 11). The concept of master numbers doesn't exist in Vedic numerology.

There is an alternate practice for dealing with master numbers 11 and 22. If an individual's number is 11, the qualities associated with number 1 are prominent and strong in him.

Chapter 11: Astro-Numerology

Both Astrology and Numerology have existed as metaphysical sciences for centuries and have been used by curious minds to get a better insight into their own lives and the lives of others. Some intrepid exponents of these fields have even made accurate predictions about future events.

Astrology has its roots dating to the second millennium BCE and can be traced to Babylon, Mesopotamia from where it spread to Egypt, Ancient Greece, Rome and gradually to Europe and from there to Arabia. Astrology is the study of the locations and movements of celestial bodies within the solar system. Based on this, astrologers prepare your natal or birth chart, which uses complicated calculations derived from the angles, degrees, house and positions of the Sun, Moon, and other relevant stars at the time of your birth to prepare a graphical chart using the sectors of a 360-degree circle.

Numerology, on the other hand, is a relatively modern discipline and is generally attributed to being conceptualized by the Greek philosopher and mathematician Pythagoras, who lived in the fifth century BCE. (Yes, the very same Pythagoras who came up with the Pythagoras Theorem, you studied in school). Pythagoras believed that each object in the universe is associated with a number, each of which has its significance. This theory was subsequently endorsed by

Einstein, who believed that each number vibrates differently and can attract both negative and positive energies and thereby affect your personality and events in life. The system propounded by Pythagoras and Einstein has been expanded endlessly in modern times and has eventually been shaped into the concepts of numerology as we know it today,

Numerology consists of five core numbers, which are the birthday, life path, personality expression and Zodiac. Of these, the most common is the "Life Path Number". To know your Life Path Number, all you require is your birthdate. You need to add the individual digits of your birth date together so that all two or over two-digit numbers are added until they result in a single-digit number. For example, let us consider the birth date, 19 June 1970 (19/6/1970).

The date of 19 will be 1 + 9, resulting in 10, which will be added as 1 + 0 = 1.

The month of June or 6 is all alone, so it will remain as 6.

The last number will be the year of birth - 1970, which will be added as 1 + 9 + 7 + 0 = 17, which will further result in 1 + 7 = 8.

The sum of the above date/month/year will add up to (1 + 6 + 8) = 15, which further leaves us with 1 + 5 = 6.

So, the Life Path Number is 6.

The above may seem pretty simple; however, there is a catch! Whenever a date, month of the year add up to 11 or 22, you do not reduce them further to single-digit numbers but retain them as they are because 11 and 22 are "master numbers" with special significance.

What does 6 as the Life Path Number signify?

Strengths of Life Path No 6: An impassioned speaker/activist, bestowed with curiosity and compassion. Ideal occupations are lawyers, orators, therapists or social services.

Challenges of Life Path Number 6: Difficulty Being Consistent

Characteristics of the Zodiac Sign – Gemini

Gemini is considered the chameleon of the Zodiac because of their ability to display different facets of themselves to the world and adapt and blend with different types of people depending on the vibes other people send out. They are also considered highly intelligent individuals who can sway people in their favor by their quick decision-making ability.

Therefore, the Life Path Number of 6 seems to indicate that the individual is a passionate activist who wishes to contribute to society and loves convincing others via his arguments. They can get along with people with different views and easily adapt themselves to any social setting. When the Life Path Number is correlated with the Zodiac, you will realize that the readings reinforce each other to give a more comprehensive picture of who you are.

An individual's Life Path Number may also list out characteristics attributed to other zodiac signs, which may probably signal the existence of an astrological alter ego. This seems very probable considering that each life path number is ruled by a specific celestial body of the solar system just like in astrology.

Once you have worked out your Life Path Number, discover which planet rules your destiny and the characteristics of your astrological alter ego.

Number 1 - Ruled by The Sun

Astrology Alter Ego: Leo

Number 1 people are always leaders, like the king of the zodiac – Leo, the lion.

Others look up to you, you are assertive and a trendsetter, whether in terms of fashion or with your bold, unique perspective on current affairs. You always take the lead, and others step in behind you.

Number 2 - Ruled by The Moon

Astrology Alter Ego: Cancer

As under the zodiac sign of Cancer, the Moon rules number two using numerology. If you are ruled by number 2, you will likely be a balanced, fair, caring and open-minded person who often acts as a mediator in feuds in your friend circle. You are the "go-to" guy who offers a patient listening to your friends and siblings and helps them sort out their issues. You are very sincere and sensitive and very affected by seeing others in distress.

Number 3 - Ruling Planet: Jupiter

Astrology Alter Ego: Sagittarius and Pisces

You are filled with creativity, imagination and energy. Mostly your passion will lie in one of the artistic disciplines, painting, writing, acting, dancing, creation, etc.

Sagittarius confers on you the ability to lucidly express your views and adapt to varied situations and people, whereas emotional sensitivity and creativity are gifts from Pisces. You are also likely to be very determined and resolute about your principles and goals.

Number 4 - Ruling Planet: Uranus

Astrology Alter Ego: Aquarius

You are likely to be unique and innovative, one who lives life by his own rules. You are not a blind follower of people, but one who is an independent thinker who makes his own decisions. You are spiritual and one who is equally comfortable amidst nature or with some of his numerous pals. You have the eye to take something simple and transform it into something grander by your signature touch. You are also diligent and have a strong intuition that helps you escape unpleasant situations.

Number 5 - Ruling Planet: Mercury

Astrology Alter Ego: Gemini, Virgo

You are intelligent, always ready with a one-liner and a witty comeback. You are the one who will always come up with a solution to an issue. Your zodiac alter ego Gemini blesses you with your enthusiastic nature and high spirits, whereas the credit for your intellect and wit should be attributed to Virgo. You are also unexpectedly grounded and despite your vivacious and free-spirited nature, you prefer to stick to familiar people and places in your life.

Number 6 - Ruling Planet: Venus

Astrology Alter Ego: Taurus, Libra

Individuals ruled by number 7 are hopeless lovers like most Taureans. They are enchanted by beauty, sensuality and romance and are always aspiring for the finer things in life.

Your easygoing and composed personality is a characteristic gifted to you by your zodiac counterpart Libra. You are a very persistent individual who follows every goal with tenacity. The most striking attribute in you is your exquisite taste.

Number 7 - Ruling Planet: Neptune

Astrology Alter Ego: Pisces

You are highly spiritual, like your ruling planet Neptune and your zodiac alter-ego Pisces. You love solitude and activities where you have the opportunity to read, research and self-reflection. You are intelligent and very knowledgeable but never use your mental facilities to impress others. You are always in support of the underdog or those who are misunderstood. You have a natural ability to understand others. Unfortunately, very few people can grasp your views on a deeper level.

Number 8 - Ruling Planet: Saturn

Astrology Alter Ego: Capricorn

You are most probably ambitious but have a soft and kind inner core under your indifferent exterior. You are very rigid and uncomfortable exploring new things. You are very sincere and dedicated. Like your zodiac counterpart Capricorn, you want balance and steadiness in your life. Emotional and financial security are very important for you in life.

Number 9 - Ruling Planet: Mars

Astrology Alter Ego: Aries, Scorpio

If ruled by number 9, you are a natural leader, confident, with a strong personality and opinion. Unfortunately, your humanitarian spirit of exploring and creating to benefit others rarely is perceived by others. You are impulsive and don't mind following your whims, even if it means going solo.

What is Astro-Numerology and what is the relation to each other?

When considered together, we realize there is a lot more in common between Astrology and Numerology than previously thought. Both rely heavily on mathematics and complex calculations to infer and explain the significance of the symbols associated with each discipline. While knowledge of mathematics and numbers is a prerequisite for preparing and interpreting a natal or birth chart, an additional understanding of planets and celestial bodies' influence enhances a numerologist's insight and interpretation of his readings. Therefore, when applied in conjunction, both astrology and numerology integrate into a fairly new field – Astro-Numerology. Astro-numerologists, whose readings are based on both astrology and numerology, have a broader picture than others who use one or the other.

Do you wonder how understanding the astro-numerology chart will help you to gain self-awareness? Your natal chart is a concise assessment of your desires, aptitudes, dreams and your life's mission. It shows you where you stand in life, the highest potential you can reach, and what you need to do to attain that potential. The five core numbers in numerology give you crucial knowledge about your purpose in life, your abilities and your inclinations. If you refer to your Astro-numerological chart when making an important decision, you can consider your strengths, inclinations, weaknesses and your purpose in life. The subsequent decision you make will be an informed one in line with the numbers, resulting in the most favorable outcome in life.

Most people who lack conviction and are not sure of their purpose in life, often live their lives as per the dictates of others or merely doing what they consider their obligations in life. Such people fail to achieve their true dharma or purpose in life and remain uncontended all their lives, chasing the dreams of others rather than their own. However, if you know your life's mission and have a strong sense of self and awareness about what you are capable of, you will not be swayed by what people say or think about you. Your self-confidence will not be affected by the labels that people attempt to slap on you because your conviction in yourself will help you overcome these obstacles and criticisms. What you think and assume becomes a reality for you. For example, even if you had the inclination and the talent to be a great artist, but you are not convinced of your ability or are dissuaded by others, you cannot succeed or find satisfaction in your life's calling. However, if backed by the data from your natal chart, and you are convinced of your artistic ability, you will be motivated to devote more attention to your passion with gusto. In this manner, awareness about numerology can help you take advantage of your strengths and achieve greater self-awareness, confidence and success, leading eventually to self-contentment and fulfillment in life.

If you have ever felt disconnected from your zodiac sign or wish to get a deeper insight into what the stars foretell, Astro-Numerology may probably have the answer to your questions. Give it a try!

Chapter 12: Tarot and Numerology

Tarot is a study of cards that are used to predict the future. Numerology is the study of energy vibrations associated with specific numbers and their connectivity. The philosophy of both these concepts dates to thousands of years, yet they are connected. The tarot deck contains 78 cards, and each card has its own meanings, symbolism and imagery. Don't get worried that you have to learn about all the 78 cards. Once you go through the information in this section, you will discover that understanding tarot is simple. These 78 cards are divided into two major categories known as Minor Arcana and Major Arcana. The Major Arcana includes 22 cards that represent significant life lessons, including spiritual ones. The other cards are the Minor Arcana and are divided into four suits of 14 cards each.

In a tarot reading, the properties of the cards suit, imagery and life lessons are combined to understand whether the individual is on the path toward self-discovery and self-development or not. It also helps ascertain if there are any possible challenges and hurdles the individual needs to overcome while working toward their goals. Tarot can be used to understand what fortune the future has in store for you or what happened in the past. Others think of it as a tool for self-reflection.

Major Arcana Cards

The significant archetypal themes in life are associated with the Major Arcana cards. Whether it is about karmic influences or life lessons, you can know more about them with Major Arcana cards. All the significant changes and transformations in life, whether good or bad, can be understood by using these cards. They are also known as trump cards. They often set the tone for a tarot reading because all the other cards will reflect the core Major Arcana cards' dominant energy.

The Major Arcana cards consist of 21 numbered cards and one unnumbered card (the fool), and they are as follows.

- The fool
- The magician
- The high priestess
- The Empress
- The emperor
- The hierophant
- The lovers
- The chariot
- Strength (known as Justice in some decks)
- The home at
- Wheel of fortune
- Justice (known as Strength in some decks)
- The hangman
- Death

- Temperance
- The devil
- The tower
- The star
- The moon
- The sun
- Judgment
- The world

Now, let's learn more about these Major Arcana cards.

The Fool

The fool is the only unnumbered card in the tarot deck. It symbolizes zero. By understanding what this card means, you understand the true power of zero. Zero is a circle, which represents totality. There is no beginning and no end to this. It is the zone of emptiness, nothingness and openness. It is purity and is defined by absence.

The Magician

The magician is a representation of creativity, the mind and attraction. Zero is nothingness, and one is about creation. Therefore, the first card of the tarot deck is where manifestation starts. One is the starting point and the first number defined. It is always about singular focus and an individual act. It can also be interpreted as of one mind and committing yourself to a specific subject without letting your attention get diverted.

The High Priestess

One is an individual, and this attracts another, which is the high priestess or number two. It is all about balance. The high priestess balances nature's opposing forces: intuition and rationality, hidden and revealed meanings, and the inner and outer worlds. It's about polarity and unity. It means two individuals are coming together to form a complete persona. Two is about expansion. This might suggest the saying two heads are better than one. Whether it is an idea or a business venture, it symbolizes the start of something new and exciting.

The Empress

A third factor that breaks the tools' polarity is introduced, and this is where the Empress steps into the picture. She is a representation of expansion and abundance. This expresses all the effort you made in the previous number. Since you've worked on attracting resources and abundance into your life along with progress, it is time to set certain limits and boundaries. Boundaries, structure and protection are important to safeguard your resources and make the most of them. If you have amassed wealth, the next step is to define what you want to do with that and how you decide.

The Emperor

The boundaries mentioned in the previous step can be set with this number. The Emperor is the representation of protection and strength. He's the overseer and the Guardian of all your resources and keeps them in order. This is the point of balance in the tarot. Nothing in life can exist if it isn't balanced. The energy given out by 2's is balanced by 4.

The Hierophant

This card is the representation of growth and challenge. If twos are the legs of wood and 4 is the table that rests on them, 5 is the challenger conflict, which senses shakes in the table. Complacency kills growth and development. You cannot grow in life without conflicts, and this is where the hierophant steps into the picture. Instead of getting too used to comforts, the hierophant challenges you to live up to higher standards and strive for something better. Five is also associated with the pentacles of Minor Arcana suits. Therefore, it is the combination of four important elements - water, fire, air and earth. Even though this card is viewed as a disruption, it ushers in growth.

The Lovers

The sixth card of the Major Arcana is the lovers. It is all about balance and harmony. If there is an excess disruption in your life, everything becomes chaotic, and there is another need for balance. The Lovers card brings this balance. It is considered a mystical number that is a true embodiment of the union between the divine feminine and masculine energies.

The Chariot

The seventh card of the Major Arcana deck is a representation of healing, spirituality and growth. This number awakens any dormant desires present within. It challenges you to pursue your goals and suggest more to life than you are looking at. It encourages you to ask important questions to make the required changes to move ahead in life. Therefore, this is the card that makes you chase your dreams. However, before you do that, it's time for a little self-introspection. Self-introspection helps you understand what you want and the reasons for the same. Once you know the destination, it becomes easier to plan the required course of action.

Strength (Also Known as Justice in Some Decks)

This card is all about balance and Infinity. Given its shape, it signifies Infinity. It is hard to determine where the number 8 starts and ends. It conveys the message that in life, everything always comes to a full circle. If it doesn't, it means there is more in store for you. It is also associated with stability, a secure foundation and abundance. In some interpretations, it is believed to be the fall of the year. Number 2 is about unity and polarity, while 4 is about protection, sturdiness and stability. Since number 8 is the combination of 2 multiplied 4, all these wonderful traits are welcome into your life by it.

The Hermit

The hermit is representative of expansion and advancement. It is also believed to be a number associated with mysticism. Since 3 represents mysticism and 9 is 3 * 3, its significance further intensified. This card encourages you to set out on a powerful journey where transformation is the goal. It helps you advance spiritually and even ideologically. By channeling your inner power, it enables you to set out on a unique path. It's commonly misunderstood that the hermit is a representation of loneliness. Instead, the hermit teaches you to be at peace with yourself. Being alone differs from loneliness. By understanding this difference, it becomes easier to tread on the path less traveled in life.

Wheel of Fortune

The wheel of fortune is a representation of completion and renewal. If one is the beginning, 10 is completion. Ten is nothing but a combination of one and zero. These are two powerful numbers. When the fool and the magician come together, it becomes the wheel of fortune. It also suggests nothing is impossible if this card shows up in your deck.

You don't have to learn about all the 22 Major Arcana cards. Instead, learning about the first ten cards will do for now. The information you obtain from the single-digit Major Arcana cards can be used to understand the double-digit ones. To keep things simple, merely add the numbers on the double-digit cards and reduce them to a single digit. Here is a simple example to clarify things.

The Star is the 17th Major Arcana card. When you reduce it to a single digit, you get 8. The 8th Major Arcana card is strength. While you experiment with different cards, you will notice certain interconnections between them. For instance, the imagery of the Lovers card is like the devil card. The devil card is believed to be the inverse of the Lovers card. Well, this isn't a coincidence. The Lovers card is the 6th Major Arcana card, and the devil is the 15th. This shows the numerical link between different cards in tarot. When the Lovers card is imbalanced, it becomes the devil card.

Minor Arcana Cards

There are 56 Minor Arcana cards used to understand more about one's trials and tribulations daily. Even though the word minor is used to describe these cards, it doesn't mean they have no effect on your life. It merely means they refer to the instances and happening in your daily life. To gain more insight into your current situation, understand any obstacle standing in your way and work on manifesting your goals, it's important to understand your Minor Arcana tarot cards. The influence associated with the Minor Arcana is believed to be temporary. It essentially means as you progress through life, the energy they give changes based on the actions you take.

A tarot reading of Minor Arcana cards helps you understand what is happening in your life right now. It gives a better insight into how the happenings of your daily life are influencing you. These offer insight into your thoughts, emotions, interactions with others and experiences as you go through life. The previous section mentioned that Major Arcana helps you understand the primary life lesson you are learning right now. The Minor Arcana cards will show the situation you are dealing with right now that's helping you learn the lesson. Even though the situation is temporary, it has immense potential to alter the course of your life.

The four suits of Minor Arcana cards are as follows.

The Suit of Wands

It represents your energy levels, passion and motivation. In a tarot reading, these cards appear when you want to know about your life purpose, contact your spirituality or work on new ideas. The element they are associated with is fire.

The Suit of Swords

In your words, actions and thoughts these are represented by the suit of swords. If these cards show up in a tarot reading, it is a sign you need to work on communicating all your wonderful ideas when you want to assert your independence and power and while making decisions. The element they are associated with is air.

The Suit of Cups

Your intuition, creativity, feelings and emotions are represented by the suit of cups. During a tarot reading about your emotional connection and relationships with yourself and others around you, these cards will come up. The element they are associated with is water.

The Suit of Pentacles

A suit of pentacles is the embodiment of all your material possessions, your finances and your career. Any tarot reading associated with your career or work and finances will include the suit of pentacles. The element they are associated with is earth.

Each of these four suits contains 14 cards. Each suit contains cards numbered through one to 10 and 4 face cards. Now, let's look at the meanings of the numbered cards in Minor Arcana.

Number 1

The number one or an ace in the tarot is the indication of something new. If there are aces in your reading, it means something new with immense potential is awaiting you in life. This represents pure energy that has no shape or home right now. Instead, this energy can be easily molded and brought to life, depending on your needs and requirements. It brings with it immense opportunities on which you can capitalize. Since the energy is raw, it is also unstable. If you don't take charge of it immediately, it will quickly overwhelm you.

Number 2

It represents pairs. It is all about unions and all the complexities involved in them. If one is about individuality, two is about pairs. According to tarot readings, number two is a representation of peace and harmony. It essentially means two opposite are coming together for the sake of creation. The balance put forth by this number might feel quite perfect. It brings with it a sense of comfort. These two factors put together can make it difficult to move forward. It can also result in difficulty when it is time to make decisions.

Number 3

Everything about group dynamics is depicted by the number 3. When a group comes together, there are different outcomes possible. Groups don't necessarily refer to individuals; they can also be ideas, opportunities or thoughts. It is also a symbolic representation of completion. In some tarot readings, it is believed that the number 3 suggests completion of the first phase.

Number 4

This number suggests there's a foundation laid down, and it is time to build on it. The primary message this number conveys is that it is time to grow and evolve in life. Unless you build and develop on the foundation, your efforts will lead to no fruition. Perhaps there were some disappointments along the way, or maybe things didn't go as planned. Regardless of the reason, number 4 in the Tarot is the universe's way of pushing you forward.

Number 5

Fives in tarot suggest change, conflict and fluctuations in life. Fives magnify the energy given out by fours. This energy encourages you to look within yourself to find the different reasons progress is important for you. So, it becomes easier to move forward despite any instability that comes your way.

Number 6

The previous number represented conflicts, while this number gives the momentum required to move away from the conflict and reach a solution. Whether or not the conflict is an internal or external one, number 6 helps find a solution. This is a card that symbolizes light after darkness.

Number 7

This number represents self-introspection and self-reflection. If sevens show up in your tarot reading, it means it's time to step back and reflect upon whatever is happening in your life. It helps reevaluate whether or not you are on the right path by assessing what you need and where you are headed. It helps you get in touch with your authentic self.

Number 8

Previously, it was mentioned that number 3 is a representation of the completion of the first phase. Number 8 is the representation of the completion of the second phase. It usually coincides with some form of achievement, whether emotional, spiritual or physical. It is an indication of growth, and it often comes in the forms we least expect.

Number 9

If number 9 shows up in your tarot reading, it means you are quite close to completion. If you are working hard on a goal, number nine suggests you are quite close to achieving it. It may also be a representation you have reached or hit a plateau and life. Even though the finishing line is near, it feels as if you have made no progress. This is the pause that comes right before a cycle and.

Number 10

Number 10 is the representation of completion of the third and final phase. This is when all your goals come to fruition. It indicates you have completed a circle, and it's time to begin again.

In tarot, the cards matter more than the numbers with which they are associated. However, numbers are helpful if you want to better understand what the cards represent. Associating numbers with the Minor Arcana is straightforward. Each number has a specific story to tell, and they play out in different ways depending on the suit they belong to.

Combining the information about individual numbers and the different suits makes it easy to understand what the tarot cards mean. For instance, let's consider the Five of Cups. Five represents love, and cups are associated with relationships. If you draw the five of cups, the tarot reading is telling you something about your love and relationships. Similarly, the five of pentacles suggests a change in association with your finances and material possessions.

Besides all the numbered cards in the Minor Arcana, there are 16 face cards of the tarot, which are known as court cards. There are four face cards present in each of the four suits in Minor Arcana. The face cards are the Page, Knight, King and the Queen. Each of these face cards shows specific energy given by the suit in the hands of different people. A simple analogy is to think of these cards as representing different stages of life. For instance, the pages are curious like children while the knights are teens or young adults, The Kings are highly skilled and grown adults while the Queens represent older and wiser figures with a deeper understanding of life. These stages can also be the journey an individual goes through in life. Everything starts with a self-development goal, an early stage, a midpoint and the end.

By understanding what the numbers mean, the representation of energy given out by different suits, and the meaning of the face cards, you can get an effective reading of an individual from their Minor Arcana cards.

The Connection Between Tarot and Numerology

There is a fascinating relationship between Major Arcana cards and the numerological life path numbers. To calculate your life part number, you need to reduce the number of your full birth date into a single digit. For instance, if an individual was born on 12.02.2001, the life path number will be 8. In the Major Arcana cards, the Birth Card is like the Life Path Number. The eight Major Arcana cards are Justice. The traits embodied by this card will correspond with the traits associated with number 8 in numerology and the Justice card in tarot. By using a combination of this, you can obtain a wealth of information about an individual's strengths and challenges. It can also be used to obtain insight into what the future holds in store for him on personal and professional fronts.

Numerology might not encompass everything tarot includes, but it can be used as a guiding tool. Tarot reading and numerological analysis go hand in hand.

Conclusion

By learning about numerology, you will finally understand the intricate relationship between science and spirituality. It proves the existence of tangibility and logic, and metaphysics. People often ask these questions on the path to self-discovery. This will act as a guide that helps you to put together the puzzle of your life. Since their discovery thousands of years ago, these concepts have been proven repeatedly. Numbers come with their own set of energy. These energies tend to influence our lives directly and indirectly.

You probably might have felt quite overwhelmed when you looked at the numerology chart for the first time. By now, you will have realized it is not that complicated. Its elegance lies in its simplicity. You don't have to be gifted to interpret numbers and understand their influence on you. As long as you are willing to learn, discovering the secrets of numerology is easy. In this book, you were given all the information you need to get started with the basics. It breaks down numerology and the easy-to-understand concepts. By calculating the influences of numbers in your life, it helps you understand your life's purpose. It might not necessarily change the course of your life, but it certainly helps you discover who you are. Self-discovery is essential for growth, and this is where numerology steps into the picture.

This is not a new concept, but its influence can still be felt in our lives. From calculating your life path number to your relationship number, there is a lot to discover. This is the perfect tool for self-discovery. While you work on calculating these numbers and understanding the true meaning and energies they give out, try to draw similarities you notice in your life and numerology teachings.

Now, all that's left for you to do is start charting the course of your life based on numerology. From calculating your birth date and numbers and understanding the influence of your name to calculating your life path and destiny numbers, you can discover a lot about yourself. This book will help you every step of the way. Commitment, curiosity and a willingness to learn are the only three things you need while discovering the world of numerology.

Once you are armed with these new insights, the next step is to leverage the power of numerology to create a life you desire. By embracing its power and making changes when required, you can finally connect with your true self. These refreshing and, at times, surprising discoveries will truly change your perception of yourself and life in general. So, what are you waiting for? Get started immediately!

Here's another book by Mari Silva that you might like

Your Free Gift (only available for a limited time)

Thanks for getting this book! If you want to learn more about various spirituality topics, then join Mari Silva's community and get a free guided meditation MP3 for awakening your third eye. This guided meditation mp3 is designed to open and strengthen ones third eye so you can experience a higher state of consciousness. Simply visit the link below the image to get started.

https://spiritualityspot.com/meditation

References

Aprile, C. (2017, November). It's All Connected! The Importance of Numerology in the Tarot. www.astrology.com website: https://www.astrology.com/article/its-all-connected-the-importance-of-numerology-in-the-tarot/

Bender, F. (2015, April 12). The Maturity Number. Felicia Bender website: https://feliciabender.com/the-maturity-number/

Bunn, M. (n.d.). Ayurveda & Vedic Science: The Science of Life. markbunn.com.au website: https://markbunn.com.au/blog/ayurveda-vedic-science-the-science-of-life

Felicia. (2017, March 23). What Your Destiny Number Reveals About Your Life Purpose. Felicia Bender website: https://feliciabender.com/the-destiny-or-expression-number/

Galbraith, A. (2019, December 19). How to find your personal year number. Where She Grows website: https://whereshegrows.com/how-to-find-your-personal-year-number/

Kuna, N. (n.d.). The 9-Year Cycle in Numerology. NATALIA KUNA: Psychic & Energy Healer. Founder of "Spiritual Course Academy" (coming soon). https://www.nataliakuna.com/ website: https://www.nataliakuna.com/the-9-year-cycle-in-numerology.html

Lad, V. (2019). Ayurveda: A Brief Introduction and Guide. Ayurveda.com website: https://www.ayurveda.com/resources/articles/ayurveda-a-brief-introduction-and-guide

Overview of Astronumerology. (n.d.). Astronumerology Wisdom website: https://www.astronumerologywisdom.com/overview-of-astronumerology.html

Numerology. (n.d.). The Meaning Of The Name website: https://themeaningofthename.com/numerology-calculator/

Numerology Of Your Birth Date – Your Destiny Decoded In Your Life Path. (n.d.). Kari Samuels website: https://karisamuels.com/life-path-number/

Numerology Calculator: Your Life Path Number And Meaning. (2015, December 15). The Law Of Attraction website: https://www.thelawofattraction.com/life-path-number-challenges/

Numerology: History, Origins, & More - Astrology.com. (2019). Astrology.com website: https://www.astrology.com/numerology

Numerology + Life Cycles. (n.d.). Flow and feels website: https://flowandfeels.com/blog/numerology-life-cycles

Samuels, K. (n.d.). Numerology Of Your Name – Your Destiny Decoded. Kari Samuels website: https://karisamuels.com/numerology-of-your-name/

The Connection Between Numerology And Astrology - Astroyogi.com. (n.d.). www.astroyogi.com website: https://www.astroyogi.com/articles/the-connection-between-numerology-and-astrology.aspx

Wilson, T. (2007, March 28). How Numerology Works. HowStuffWorks website: https://science.howstuffworks.com/science-vs-myth/extrasensory-perceptions/numerology.htm

Printed in Great Britain
by Amazon